How to Love Myself

CRAFTED BY SKRIUWER

Copyright © 2024 by Skriuwer.

All rights reserved. No part of this book may be used or reproduced in any form whatsoever without written permission except in the case of brief quotations in critical articles or reviews.

For more information, contact : **kontakt@skriuwer.com** (www.skriuwer.com)

TABLE OF CONTENTS

CHAPTER 1: THE NEED FOR SELF-ACCEPTANCE

- *What self-acceptance really means and why it matters*
- *How low self-worth forms and ways to address it*
- *Recognizing common obstacles to liking yourself*

CHAPTER 2: UNDERSTANDING NEGATIVE SELF-TALK

- *Identifying harmful thought patterns*
- *Challenging and replacing negative inner messages*
- *Turning harsh self-criticism into balanced thinking*

CHAPTER 3: BUILDING A NEW VIEW OF YOURSELF

- *Breaking free from old labels and beliefs*
- *Seeing both strengths and areas to grow*
- *Practical steps to shape a healthier self-image*

CHAPTER 4: LEARNING TO LET GO OF SHAME

- *How shame can block self-acceptance*
- *Gentle methods to face and release deep regrets*
- *Replacing shame with more supportive inner responses*

CHAPTER 5: SELF-WORTH AND CONFIDENCE

- *Differences between self-worth and skill-based confidence*
- *How to nurture a strong sense of internal value*
- *Overcoming fear of failure through self-belief*

CHAPTER 6: THE POWER OF SETTING BOUNDARIES

- *Understanding healthy limits in relationships*
- *Protecting your space, time, and emotional energy*
- *Communicating limits calmly and standing firm*

CHAPTER 7: HEALTHY RELATIONSHIPS

- *Key features of caring, respectful connections*
- *Avoiding toxic patterns and nurturing genuine support*
- *Handling disagreements without harming self-esteem*

CHAPTER 8: RESPECT FOR YOUR BODY

- *Strengthening the mind-body link for overall well-being*
- *Basic steps to care for physical health and boost self-image*
- *Overcoming negative body thoughts or habits*

CHAPTER 9: MANAGING STRESS AND WORRY

- *Common sources of stress and how they affect you*
- *Practical ways to lower tension and calm the mind*
- *Shifting from constant worry to confident problem-solving*

CHAPTER 10: PERSONAL VALUES

- *Defining what truly matters to you*
- *Aligning decisions and daily life with core beliefs*
- *Finding purpose and direction through clear values*

TABLE OF CONTENTS

CHAPTER 1: THE NEED FOR SELF-ACCEPTANCE

- *What self-acceptance really means and why it matters*
- *How low self-worth forms and ways to address it*
- *Recognizing common obstacles to liking yourself*

CHAPTER 2: UNDERSTANDING NEGATIVE SELF-TALK

- *Identifying harmful thought patterns*
- *Challenging and replacing negative inner messages*
- *Turning harsh self-criticism into balanced thinking*

CHAPTER 3: BUILDING A NEW VIEW OF YOURSELF

- *Breaking free from old labels and beliefs*
- *Seeing both strengths and areas to grow*
- *Practical steps to shape a healthier self-image*

CHAPTER 4: LEARNING TO LET GO OF SHAME

- *How shame can block self-acceptance*
- *Gentle methods to face and release deep regrets*
- *Replacing shame with more supportive inner responses*

CHAPTER 5: SELF-WORTH AND CONFIDENCE

- *Differences between self-worth and skill-based confidence*
- *How to nurture a strong sense of internal value*
- *Overcoming fear of failure through self-belief*

CHAPTER 6: THE POWER OF SETTING BOUNDARIES

- *Understanding healthy limits in relationships*
- *Protecting your space, time, and emotional energy*
- *Communicating limits calmly and standing firm*

CHAPTER 7: HEALTHY RELATIONSHIPS

- *Key features of caring, respectful connections*
- *Avoiding toxic patterns and nurturing genuine support*
- *Handling disagreements without harming self-esteem*

CHAPTER 8: RESPECT FOR YOUR BODY

- *Strengthening the mind-body link for overall well-being*
- *Basic steps to care for physical health and boost self-image*
- *Overcoming negative body thoughts or habits*

CHAPTER 9: MANAGING STRESS AND WORRY

- *Common sources of stress and how they affect you*
- *Practical ways to lower tension and calm the mind*
- *Shifting from constant worry to confident problem-solving*

CHAPTER 10: PERSONAL VALUES

- *Defining what truly matters to you*
- *Aligning decisions and daily life with core beliefs*
- *Finding purpose and direction through clear values*

CHAPTER 11: SETTING REALISTIC GOALS

- *Why balanced, achievable aims are crucial*
- *Breaking big dreams into smaller, workable steps*
- *Staying motivated and handling setbacks*

CHAPTER 12: BREAKING OLD PATTERNS

- *Why unwanted habits persist and how to replace them*
- *Methods to spot triggers and choose better responses*
- *Creating a supportive environment to avoid slipping back*

CHAPTER 13: BUILDING GOOD HABITS

- *Turning small daily actions into lasting routines*
- *Finding enjoyment in repetition and progress*
- *Sticking to new habits through planning and rewards*

CHAPTER 14: OVERCOMING FEAR

- *Recognizing fear and its effects on self-esteem*
- *Gradual steps to face what scares you*
- *Replacing "What if I fail?" with "I can try and learn"*

CHAPTER 15: THE IMPORTANCE OF FORGIVENESS

- *Distinguishing forgiveness from approval or weakness*
- *Releasing anger toward others or yourself*
- *Finding emotional freedom through genuine letting go*

CHAPTER 16: FINDING HOPE IN HARD TIMES

- *Holding on to optimism when life feels heavy*
- *Small actions that keep you going through setbacks*
- *Balancing acceptance of reality with belief in solutions*

CHAPTER 17: DAILY ACTIONS FOR GROWTH

- *How simple routines shape self-improvement*
- *Making small efforts that add up over time*
- *Adapting daily habits when life changes*

CHAPTER 18: LEARNING FROM MISTAKES

- *Turning errors into guides for progress*
- *Healthy ways to respond without shame*
- *Apologizing, making amends, and moving forward*

CHAPTER 19: PUTTING KINDNESS INTO PRACTICE

- *Showing care to others and yourself in balanced ways*
- *Knowing the difference between kindness and people-pleasing*
- *Spreading warmth and positivity in daily life*

CHAPTER 20: LONG-TERM STRATEGIES

- *Maintaining self-growth through life's changes*
- *Reviewing goals, adjusting habits, and seeking fresh support*
- *Staying resilient with hope, kindness, and self-acceptance for the future*

CHAPTER 1: THE NEED FOR SELF-ACCEPTANCE

It is common for people of all ages to wonder if they are good enough. Many people feel a sense of worry about how others see them. They might also think poorly of themselves without fully understanding why. Some people feel sad because they never stop to see their own good points. This first chapter is about why it is important to take care of your feelings toward yourself. We will look at how low self-worth can harm your life, and why it is worth it to work on how you feel about yourself.

What Does Self-Acceptance Mean?

Self-acceptance means being okay with who you are. It does not mean you think you are perfect. It just means you are willing to see yourself clearly—both your strong points and weak points—without being too hard on yourself. People often mix up self-acceptance with bragging or thinking you are better than others. That is not what self-acceptance is about. Self-acceptance is more like saying, "I see who I am right now, and I am fine with that, even if there are areas I want to improve."

Many people feel pressure to act a certain way to be liked. They see ads or people on social media who seem perfect. They might think something is wrong with them if they do not look or act like those people. That can be a huge load to carry. When you accept yourself, you are no longer controlled by the need to fit a certain standard. Instead, you can say, "I am who I am, and that is okay."

Why Is Self-Acceptance So Important?

Self-acceptance can affect many parts of your life. When you have a healthy sense of yourself, you can handle stress better. You are less likely to feel small when something does not go your way. You can see a problem as just that—a problem—rather than a sign that you are not good enough. This can help you think more clearly and find smart ways to fix the issue.

Self-acceptance also helps you stay true to your own values. If you do not accept yourself, you might go along with what other people want, even if it makes you feel uneasy. For example, you might say yes to a friend who wants you to do something you do not enjoy, just to feel liked. But if you accept yourself, you can stand firm in your choices. This can lead to deeper respect for yourself, which in turn helps others respect you too.

Another reason self-acceptance is vital is that it supports mental health. People who are hard on themselves often feel stressed, sad, or anxious. Over time, these feelings can get worse. However, when you learn to be okay with who you are, these painful feelings might happen less often or carry less weight. That does not mean problems disappear, but it means you have a better way to handle them.

Common Obstacles to Self-Acceptance

Before we go further, it is helpful to see what usually stands in the way of liking who you are:

1. **Social Pressure**: Ads often show people who look a certain way, such as super thin or wearing expensive clothes. This can make people think that if they do not fit that look, they are not good enough. Over time, these messages can wear down your sense of worth.
2. **Family Background**: Some families encourage achievement in a way that makes a child feel they must be perfect. If a parent or caregiver only shows approval when a child meets high marks or wins an award, that child may grow up feeling they are only worthy if they meet those high standards. This can cause problems later in life.
3. **Fear of Failure**: Many people avoid new tasks or goals because they are afraid of messing up. They worry that making a mistake will prove they are not smart or capable. This fear can keep them from

accepting themselves. In reality, making mistakes is a normal part of learning.
4. **Comparing to Others**: A lot of us compare ourselves to friends, coworkers, or even strangers on social media. It is not always a bad thing to notice what others are doing, but constant comparison can make you feel less worthy. Each person has a different path, and it is not fair to judge yourself by someone else's strengths or surface appearance.
5. **Past Failures**: If you have faced rejection or letdown in the past, you might think that pattern will continue. This can lead to a sense that you are not good enough to succeed. But past events do not have to rule your future.

The Impact of Not Accepting Yourself

If you do not accept yourself, you may see problems in many areas of your life. It can affect your work, relationships, and even your day-to-day mood. You might feel a never-ending sense that something is lacking. Here are some ways that a lack of self-acceptance can show up:

- **Trouble Making Choices**: When you do not trust yourself, you may find it hard to decide. You might wait for others to tell you what to do because you are worried you will choose wrong.
- **Feeling Overly Guilty**: Guilt can be helpful in showing us when we have hurt someone or broken a moral rule. But if you do not accept yourself, you might feel guilty for small things. You might blame yourself for things that are outside your control.
- **Difficulty in Friendships**: It is hard to be open with friends if you think they will judge you. This can lead to shallow friendships that never reach real closeness.
- **Low Energy**: Constantly feeling down about yourself can drain your energy. You might find it hard to get out of bed or do daily tasks. This is because so much mental energy is spent on negative thoughts.
- **Increased Stress**: If you do not accept yourself, your stress levels might be high. Every time you face a challenge, you might see it as a

personal failure rather than a normal part of life. This stress can lead to physical problems, such as headaches or trouble sleeping.

Recognizing the Signs

Some people may not even be aware that they are not accepting themselves. They might walk around feeling like something is wrong but not be sure what it is. Recognizing the signs is the first step. Some signs include:

- You talk to yourself harshly, using words like "stupid" or "worthless" when you make mistakes.
- You feel envy when someone else does well, because you see it as proof you are not good enough.
- You often worry about how you appear to others, and you change how you act to get approval.
- You fear trying new things because you think you will fail.

Not everyone shows these signs in the same way. Some people might try to hide their feelings by acting overly positive. Others might say they do not care about anything. But deep down, they might still feel insecure.

Steps Toward Self-Acceptance

1. **Notice Your Thoughts**: The first step is to become aware of the messages you tell yourself each day. If you find yourself thinking, "I am so clumsy," pause and consider if that is fair. Is it based on facts, or is it a habit of criticizing yourself?
2. **Consider Your Achievements**: Make a simple list of things you have done well. These can be big or small. Maybe you helped a friend who was sad, or you learned a new skill. Keep this list in a place where you can see it often, so you remember your strengths.
3. **Separate Mistakes from Who You Are**: Failing at a task does not mean you are a bad person. It only means there is a skill or action

you have not mastered yet. Learn to view mistakes as normal rather than proof of your worth.
4. **Seek Helpful Support**: If possible, find people who show kindness and respect for you. This can be a friend, a teacher, a counselor, or a close relative. The right people in your life can help you see your good points when you lose sight of them.
5. **Learn to Let Go of Criticism**: If someone criticizes you in a way that is not helpful, try not to let it sink in. Learn to tell the difference between helpful feedback and harsh judgment. Helpful feedback points out something specific you can improve, while harsh judgment tears you down as a person.

A Helpful Tip for Growth

Here is a technique that many people find useful. It is simple enough for a child or teen but also works for adults. Take a small piece of paper or a sticky note. Write one positive fact about yourself on it. It could be, "I am kind to animals," or, "I am a caring friend." Then place that note on your mirror or on a spot you see every day. This does two things: it reminds you of a good fact you might forget, and it helps shift the way you think about yourself over time.

Sometimes, you might feel awkward doing this. That is normal. But over time, these positive reminders can chip away at years of negative thoughts that have built up in your mind.

A Different Way to See Yourself

Many people measure their worth by their achievements, looks, or social status. But there is more to you than any single role. Think about the different parts of your life—family, friends, hobbies, personal values, and so on. If you do not do well in one area, it does not mean you are a failure in everything. By spreading out your sense of worth, you will not feel like the floor drops out from under you if one thing goes wrong.

For example, suppose you are learning to play a sport, and you make a mistake in a game. That does not mean you are useless as a person. Maybe you are also kind to your neighbors, or you write good stories, or you are good at helping classmates when they struggle. One bad moment in one area does not define you.

How to Keep Moving Forward

Self-acceptance is not something you achieve once and then forget about. It is an ongoing process. Life will bring new challenges and changes. You might feel strong about yourself for a while, and then something happens—like losing a job or having a fight with a friend—and suddenly your self-worth drops again. That is okay. It is part of life to go up and down. The key is to remember you have the power to choose how you see yourself.

Here are some ways to keep up the progress:

- **Check in with Yourself Regularly**: Once a week, ask yourself how you feel about who you are. Are there areas you feel good about? Are there areas you are worried about?
- **Practice Acts of Kindness**: Doing kind acts can remind you that you have value. But do not do these acts just to prove your worth. Do them because they match what you believe is good.
- **Stay Alert to Negative Talk**: If you notice you are speaking harshly to yourself again, see it as a small alarm. Then try to correct that talk.

Points That Go Beyond the Usual

Many people will say, "Be nicer to yourself." But there are some lesser-known approaches to build self-acceptance in a more solid way:

1. **Learn About Your Family Patterns**: Sometimes, the way we see ourselves is passed down from parents or grandparents. If your parents were very critical, you might have learned to be tough on

yourself. By understanding this, you can see that your self-view might be a habit you picked up, rather than a fact about who you are.
2. **Check the Source of Your Information**: If you catch yourself thinking, "I am not capable," ask, "Where did I get that idea?" You might find it is from an offhand remark someone made years ago. Once you see how weak that source is, you can let go of that thought more easily.
3. **Try Small Challenges and Track the Results**: Pick a small goal that you can do in a week or so. It could be reading a short book or completing a puzzle. Write down the steps you took, how you felt, and what you learned about yourself. Doing this can give you clear proof that you can handle new tasks, and it fights the idea that you cannot do anything right.
4. **Look at Areas You Avoid**: Sometimes, we avoid tasks that scare us, like public speaking or making new friends. Ask yourself why. Then, see if there is a simple way to step closer to that area. You do not have to leap into it at once. Maybe you can practice in front of one friend before speaking in front of a larger group. Bit by bit, you can lessen the fear and see that you can handle more than you thought.

These ideas can be very helpful because they go deeper than the usual advice. They help you see exactly how certain beliefs formed and how you can replace them.

Practical Exercise: The "Fair Friend" Test

When you feel unsure about yourself, try this quick test: Ask yourself, "Would I talk to a friend the same way I am talking to myself right now?" Usually, the answer is no. For example, if a friend forgot to pay a bill on time, would you call them "worthless"? Of course not. You might remind them to be more careful next time, but you would not see them as a failure. So why treat yourself any worse?

By asking this question, you put yourself in a more balanced mindset. You realize you deserve the same fairness and understanding you would offer someone else.

Closing Thoughts on Self-Acceptance

Self-acceptance is a key piece of feeling at peace with yourself and growing in other areas of life. When you are okay with who you are, you have a solid base. You can still make changes or improvements, but you do not see it as trying to fix a broken person. Instead, you see it as learning and growing, which everyone does.

In the next chapters, we will look at more ways to make your self-talk healthier, to handle shame, and to protect your sense of worth. For now, remember that self-acceptance is not about giving up on improving yourself. It is about seeing yourself as worthy and capable, right where you are.

CHAPTER 2: UNDERSTANDING NEGATIVE SELF-TALK

Negative self-talk is the voice in your head that tells you, "You can't do anything right," or "No one likes you." It is like having a harsh critic living inside your mind. This chapter will explain how that voice forms, why it sticks around, and what you can do to change it. Negative self-talk can be very powerful, but there are ways to reduce its impact.

What Is Negative Self-Talk?

Negative self-talk is any thought pattern that brings you down and makes you feel bad about yourself. It might sound like, "I always mess up," "I am so lazy," or "Nothing good ever happens to me." The more you repeat these thoughts, the stronger they become. You might start to believe them as if they are facts.

Many people do not even realize they are talking to themselves in a negative way. These thoughts may have started in childhood and continued into adult life. But recognizing that you have these thoughts is the first step to dealing with them.

Different Types of Negative Self-Talk

Negative self-talk comes in many forms. Here are some common examples:

1. **All-or-Nothing Thinking**: This is when you see things in black and white. For instance, if you do not complete a task perfectly, you think you have failed completely. There is no room for "I did okay" or "I can try again."

2. **Overgeneralizing**: This happens when you take one negative event and make it into a pattern. You forget that one bad day does not mean every day will be bad.
3. **Ignoring the Positive**: Even when you do something well, you might say it was just luck or that it does not matter. You focus only on the parts you did not do well, ignoring any praise or achievement.
4. **Self-Blame**: You blame yourself for problems that are not really your fault. If a friend is in a bad mood, you might think, "I must have done something wrong to cause this," even when there is no proof of that.
5. **Mind-Reading**: This is when you assume you know what other people think about you, and it is usually something negative like "They must think I'm boring."

Learning to spot these patterns can help you correct them. Once you notice them, you can pause and say, "Wait, am I being fair to myself here?"

Why Negative Self-Talk Feels So Real

You might wonder why these thoughts seem so convincing. The brain looks for patterns as a way to make sense of life. If you have repeated "I'm not good enough" many times, your brain will look for proof of that idea. You might ignore any evidence that shows you are capable and zero in on small mistakes instead. This creates a loop that is hard to break.

Social pressure and certain experiences can add to this loop. If you grew up with a critical parent, you might have heard negative messages often. Over time, these messages can become your own thoughts. Or, if you were bullied at school, you might start to believe the hurtful words others said about you. The human mind can stick to old messages, even when they no longer match reality.

The Effects of Negative Self-Talk

Negative self-talk can impact many parts of your life. Here are just a few examples:

- **Lower Self-Worth**: Constantly putting yourself down leads to feeling unworthy. You start to believe you do not deserve good things, which can make you hold back from trying to improve your life.
- **Anxiety and Stress**: If your mind is filled with harsh thoughts, it keeps you in a state of worry. You may feel tense all the time because you are expecting something bad to happen.
- **Poor Relationships**: When you do not think well of yourself, you might push people away or act in ways that are not good for healthy friendships and relationships.
- **Lack of Motivation**: Negative self-talk can drain your energy. You may think, "What's the point in trying?" This can lead you to give up on goals or not start them in the first place.
- **Health Problems**: High stress from constant negative thinking can lead to issues like headaches, stomach pain, or trouble sleeping.

Early Warning Signs

You might wonder how you can spot negative self-talk before it takes over. One sign is a sudden shift in mood. If you wake up feeling okay but then suddenly feel sad or angry, try to see what thought caused that change. Another sign is when you use the same harsh words or phrases in your mind. Words like "never," "always," or "ugly" can be clues.

When you notice that your mood has changed quickly, pause and ask yourself what just went through your mind. Identifying that thought is the first step to stopping the loop. At first, it might be hard to catch these thoughts because they happen so fast. But with practice, you can start to notice them more often.

Ways to Challenge Negative Self-Talk

You can break free from negative self-talk by questioning it. Here are some methods:

1. **Ask for Facts**: If you think, "I always fail," ask yourself, "Is that true every single time?" You might remember many times you did not fail, which proves your thought is not correct.
2. **Think Like a Friend**: Treat yourself the way you would treat someone you care about. If a friend came to you with the same thought, what would you say to them?
3. **Write It Down**: Putting your thoughts on paper helps you see them more clearly. You can then look at the words and decide if they make sense. You might be surprised at how extreme they appear when written out.
4. **Balance with Reality**: If you find yourself thinking, "I messed up this project, so I'm useless," try to add a more balanced view: "I made a mistake on this project, but I have done other projects well. I can learn from this one and do better next time."
5. **Replace with a More True Thought**: If you have a pattern of telling yourself something that is not accurate, try replacing it with a statement that is more in line with facts. For example, change "I can't do anything right" to "I did something wrong today, but I can try again, and I might do it better."

Over time, this kind of questioning can weaken the hold of negative self-talk. It might not vanish overnight, but the intensity often goes down.

A Simple Trick for Tough Moments

Imagine you are in the middle of a strong negative thought. Maybe you just got a poor grade or made an error at work, and your mind is racing with thoughts like, "This proves I'm a failure." One trick is to pause and name the thought: "I'm having the 'I'm a failure' thought again." By labeling it, you shift your focus from the thought's content to the fact that it is just a thought. That small shift can help you see it is not a definite fact—it is a mental event passing through your mind.

This method might feel strange at first. But it can help you gain distance from thoughts that are harmful. This distance gives you a chance to think more clearly, rather than simply accepting the negative thought as the truth.

Dealing with Negative Self-Talk in the Long Term

It is one thing to handle negative thoughts in the moment, but how do you reduce them over the long term? Here are some strategies:

1. **Build a Positive Environment**: Spend time with people who are kind and uplifting. This does not mean you should avoid anyone who has problems. But try to keep a circle of support around you. If you have a friend who is always putting themselves or others down, limit how much you let those words shape your mind.
2. **Celebrate Small Wins**: Keep track of small victories, such as finishing a task you have been putting off or speaking up in a group when you usually stay quiet. Note them down somewhere so you can revisit them when negative thoughts arise.
3. **Practice Relaxation**: Techniques like slow breathing, going for walks, or listening to calm music can help lower stress. When you are less stressed, you are more able to challenge negative thoughts.
4. **Work on Specific Skills**: Sometimes negative self-talk is tied to a specific issue. If you keep thinking you are bad at math, for example, sign up for a short course or ask a friend to help you. Improving a skill can give you evidence that your old thought was not fully accurate.
5. **Seek Professional Help**: A counselor or therapist is trained to help you spot and change negative thought patterns. If negative self-talk is strong in your life, it might be worth seeking professional guidance.

Unexpected Facts That Can Help

1. **Memory Bias**: The human mind remembers negative events more strongly than positive ones. This is a survival trait from old times, when remembering dangers was key. Realizing this can help you see that your mind might be overvaluing negative data.

2. **Sound and Mood**: Studies show that certain sounds can influence your mood. Natural sounds like soft rain or a calm breeze can lessen stress in many people. If you feel stuck in negative thoughts, playing recordings of these sounds might help shift your state of mind.
3. **Body Position**: Your body stance can affect how you feel. Slouching can make negative thoughts feel stronger, while standing up straight can sometimes boost your sense of confidence. Though it may seem small, how you hold your body can impact how you think.
4. **Cognitive Defusion**: This is a tool from a kind of therapy called Acceptance and Commitment Therapy (ACT). One exercise is to say a negative thought out loud using a silly voice or sing it to a simple tune. This might sound odd, but it can help your mind see that the thought is just a group of words, not a permanent truth.

These facts are not known by everyone, and they provide a bit of insight beyond the usual advice like "think positive." Each one can help you realize that your mind and body are connected in surprising ways, and you have more tools than you might think to handle negative self-talk.

Building a Routine to Address Negative Self-Talk

One of the best ways to keep negative self-talk in check is to make a routine for checking your thoughts. Here is a simple, step-by-step routine you can do each day or week:

1. **Set Aside Time**: Choose a short period each day (maybe 5 or 10 minutes) to think about your thoughts. This might be before bed or first thing in the morning.
2. **Reflect**: Ask yourself what negative thoughts came up during the day (or the day before). Write them down if you can.
3. **Examine**: For each negative thought, ask if it was fair or if it was one of the common patterns (overgeneralizing, ignoring the positive, etc.).
4. **Correct**: Write down a more balanced thought next to the negative one. It does not have to be overly sweet, just something more realistic.

5. **Plan**: If there is a pattern that keeps popping up, think of steps to address it. For example, if you keep thinking you are disorganized, maybe you can plan a small step to organize your desk or room.

Doing this can create a habit of questioning negative self-talk. Over time, you may start doing it automatically in your head.

The Connection to Self-Acceptance

You might be wondering how negative self-talk links to the theme of self-acceptance. The answer is that negative self-talk is one of the main reasons people fail to like who they are. Even if there is no proof that you are lacking, the constant negative chatter in your mind can make you feel unworthy.

When you reduce negative self-talk, you open up space for a more fair view of who you are. You may still have things you want to change about yourself, but you will not see yourself as hopeless. This is a big step toward truly liking who you are and feeling comfortable in your own skin.

A Special Exercise: A Thought Journal

Many people have found that keeping a thought journal helps. Each day, write down a few negative thoughts that came to mind. Then try to figure out what triggered them. Did something happen at school or work? Did you see someone's post online that made you feel lacking?

Next, question the thought. Is it based on actual evidence, or is it a knee-jerk reaction? Can you think of a different way to see the same event? For instance, if your negative thought was, "My friend didn't text me back right away, so she must be mad at me," consider other reasons. Perhaps she was busy, or her phone battery died. By writing these reasons down, you teach your brain to look for balanced explanations rather than the worst-case scenario.

Being Patient with the Process

Changing negative self-talk takes time. You have to unlearn patterns that might have been in place for many years. This can lead to frustration if you expect quick results. Sometimes, it might feel like you are back to square one after a stressful day. That is normal.

Remember that every time you challenge a negative thought, you are making progress. It might not feel like a big change at first, but these small efforts add up. Over time, you will notice that harsh thoughts occur less often or carry less weight. You might also find you have more energy for other things in your life because you are not spending so much mental effort on tearing yourself down.

Mistakes Along the Way

It is important to note that you will make mistakes in this process. You might slip back into old thought habits. You might forget to do your daily check-ins. Do not see these setbacks as proof you cannot change. Instead, try to see them as part of being human. Everyone slips up sometimes. The key is to keep going.

If you feel you have completely fallen back into negative self-talk, look at it as a chance to practice the tools you have learned. Notice how you talk to yourself. Question the thoughts. Remind yourself that just because you made a mistake does not mean you have not learned anything. This step is part of building a strong base of self-acceptance.

Final Thoughts on Negative Self-Talk

Negative self-talk is a common problem. Many people of all ages struggle with that harsh inner voice. The good news is that it is possible to reduce it and replace it with more realistic, caring self-talk. This does not happen overnight, but with consistent effort, you can see real progress.

As we move ahead in this book, we will explore other topics like letting go of shame, setting boundaries, and handling worry. All these areas connect to how we see and talk to ourselves. By learning about negative self-talk now, you have taken the first big step toward building a better relationship with yourself.

Looking Forward

In the next chapters, we will look at more topics that influence how you feel about yourself. For instance, shame is closely tied to negative thoughts. If you carry shame from past mistakes or experiences, it can feed negative thinking. We will look at methods to break free from shame. We will also look at creating healthier relationships because the people around you can play a big part in how you speak to yourself.

By gaining tools for both your mind (like challenging negative thoughts) and your life (like forming positive connections), you can continue to grow. With practice, you can learn to see yourself in a more balanced light and treat yourself with kindness.

Remember: Everyone has an inner voice. The key is to shape that voice into one that helps you, rather than harms you. By challenging negative self-talk, you are making an important choice to care for yourself. This choice will pay off in better mental health, stronger friendships, and a greater sense of peace. Keep going. It is worth it.

CHAPTER 3: BUILDING A NEW VIEW OF YOURSELF

Building a new view of yourself is an important step if you want to stop harsh thoughts and feel good about who you are. In this chapter, we will look at how a person can form a healthy picture of themselves and move past old self-beliefs that keep them stuck. By the end, you should have clear steps to help you see yourself in a better light.

Why Your View of Yourself Matters

When you think about who you are, you form a personal story. If that story is full of negative points, you may feel down or even hopeless. On the other hand, if your story includes the honest truth that you have both good and bad sides, you can see yourself in a fair way. This balanced view can encourage you to work on your skills and accept your own limits without constant shame.

Your view of yourself can direct your actions each day. For example, if you believe you are too shy to speak up, you might never raise your hand in class or volunteer at work. Over time, this belief grows stronger because you see yourself avoiding these actions, which seems to prove the belief is true. But if you decide to shift that view and see yourself as someone who can learn to speak up, you can start to take small steps to test that belief. This can help you grow.

Recognizing Your Old Story

Each person has an old story about who they are. This story might include details from childhood. Maybe you were told you were not good at sports or not good at math. Maybe someone once called you a "crybaby." Even small comments from your past can shape how you see yourself years later.

To build a new view of yourself, it is helpful to first understand what your old view looks like. Take a few minutes and list words you often use to describe yourself. They could be words like "quiet," "lazy," "kind," or "anxious." Some might be positive, some negative, and some neutral. This list gives you a starting point to see which labels you have been living with, sometimes without even noticing.

Next, ask yourself where these labels came from. Did you choose them based on facts, or did someone else give them to you? Did you have one bad experience and decide you were no good in that area forever? Often, people hold on to old labels that are no longer accurate. By seeing which labels are outdated, you can begin to let them go.

Why It Is Hard to Change Old Labels

You might think, "Why not just pick new labels for myself?" It is not always that easy. Old labels stick around because:

1. **Family Beliefs**: Sometimes, families share certain views about their children. They might call one child "the brainy one" and another "the clumsy one." Even if these labels are not meant to be cruel, they can become part of your identity.
2. **Group Pressure**: You might have friends or coworkers who see you a certain way. They might tease you or treat you as if you cannot change. This can feel like a trap.
3. **Fear of New Choices**: Changing labels means trying things that might feel risky. If you have always thought you are "bad at making friends," the idea of meeting new people can feel scary. Your old label might seem safer, even though it hurts you.
4. **Proof Bias**: The mind looks for proof that matches what it already believes. So if you have labeled yourself "not creative," you might ignore the creative things you have done or could do.

Despite these hurdles, it is possible to break free. The first step is to realize that no single label can describe the whole you. We can hold many traits at once, some that are strong and some that need work.

Steps to Form a Healthier View

1. **Write a Balanced Description**: Take a piece of paper and write a simple description of yourself. Include good traits you have—maybe you are patient or funny—and also areas where you can grow, like learning to manage anger or improving study habits. The goal is not to make a perfect list, but to practice seeing both sides.
2. **Learn from Outside Feedback**: Sometimes, we do not see ourselves clearly. Ask a trusted friend or family member to share one or two positive traits they see in you. Make sure you pick someone who will speak honestly, not just flatter you. Compare what they say to how you see yourself.
3. **Look for Times You Broke the Old Pattern**: Think of a moment when you acted differently than your old label would suggest. If you used to call yourself "too shy," recall a moment you spoke up or made a new friend. Note these moments down. They show that your old label might not be the whole story.
4. **Try Something New**: Even a small new activity can help you see yourself differently. If you think you are "not athletic," try a short walk or a mild exercise routine. If you believe you "cannot cook," find a simple recipe and give it a try. Success in these small things can shake loose those old labels.
5. **Watch Your Self-Talk**: As you attempt new things, note any harsh thoughts that pop up. For instance, if you catch yourself thinking, "I can't do this," replace it with, "I can learn to do this if I give it a fair try." This shift helps you create a new story.

Surprising Insights

- **The Mind Grows with Practice**: Scientists once believed the adult brain was mostly fixed. Now we know that the brain can form new links throughout life. This is called "neuroplasticity." It means that learning a new skill or a new way of thinking is possible at any age. You are not stuck with an old label forever.

- **Self-Image and Health**: Some studies show that a negative self-image can worsen physical health problems. Stress from seeing yourself in a negative light can affect your immune system. On the other hand, a balanced view of yourself—one that allows for mistakes—can help lower stress. Good mental health habits support your overall well-being.
- **Role Models**: Seeing someone else succeed in an area you thought was closed off to you can open your eyes. If you think you are "too old" to learn something, but then see someone older than you doing it, that old label can lose its power. Seek out stories of people who break the limits you think apply to you.

Putting It into Daily Life

The process of building a new view of yourself does not happen only in your head. It needs to show up in your daily actions. For example, if you decide you are able to learn new things, show yourself that truth by picking up a new hobby. If you decide you are a caring friend, make a habit of checking in on people you care about. These actions take the idea of "a new view" and ground it in real events.

It also helps to reflect on how certain tasks or social settings make you feel about yourself. If you find that a certain group of people always makes you feel that you cannot change, it may be time to set some limits with them or spend less time around them. Not everyone will support your new view. Some may prefer you stay the same because it fits how they see the world. In those cases, you have to stand firm in your choice to change.

A Simple Method to Track Progress

Try keeping a notebook where you track any steps you take that show the new view of yourself. Write down what you did and how it felt. For instance:

- **Date**: Monday

- **Action**: Spoke up in our team meeting at work
- **Feelings**: Nervous at first, then felt proud for sharing ideas.

Looking back over these entries helps you see that you really are changing. It also keeps you motivated. If you have a day when you fall back into old thinking, you can flip through this notebook for reminders of what you can do.

Handling Setbacks

No change happens without setbacks. You might feel good about your new view for a while, and then something happens—maybe you get criticized by a boss or a friend ignores you—and suddenly you feel like you are back to your old labels. This is normal. It does not erase your progress.

When a setback occurs, try to see it as a single event instead of a complete collapse. Maybe you messed up a project. That does not mean you are forever "a failure." It just means you had trouble with that project. Check if there is something you can learn. Maybe you need more training, or you need to manage your time better. Focus on the action steps that could help next time, rather than turning it into a harsh label.

The Effect of a New View on Relationships

It might seem like building a new view is all about you, but it can also change how you relate to people around you. When you feel more balanced about who you are, you become more open to healthy friendships. You might be less defensive because you do not feel under attack all the time. You might be less needy for approval because you know your own worth.

People often notice when someone starts to act with a stronger sense of self. They might respect you more or feel calmer around you. However, be ready for some people to resist the change. This can happen if they used to feel bigger by comparing themselves to you. Keep in mind that you are allowed to grow, even if it unsettles others.

A Practice for Seeing the Good in Yourself

For one week, every night, write down one or two good things about yourself or your day. Try not to repeat the same things each time. These items can be very small, like "I stayed polite when I was stuck in a long line at the store." Over time, you might notice patterns: maybe you are helpful, maybe you stay calm under pressure, or maybe you are playful. This record can help shift your focus from your faults to your strengths. It is a slow process, but it helps train your mind to look for what is right, not just what is wrong.

Going Beyond the Basics

To deepen your new view of yourself, you can:

1. **Learn New Skills**: Perhaps you have always wanted to draw, play a musical instrument, or code a computer program. Pick a skill and watch free online videos or join a beginner group. Seeing yourself make progress can weaken old ideas that "you can't learn."
2. **Share Knowledge with Others**: If there is something you do well, teach it to someone else. You may start to see yourself as skilled and helpful, which can contrast with an old label like "useless."
3. **Try New Social Circles**: If your old social group keeps putting you in a box, meet new people who do not know your old labels. Sometimes, a fresh environment can help you step into a healthier view of yourself.
4. **Read or Watch Success Stories**: If you read about or watch interviews with people who have overcome big obstacles, you might notice that they had to change how they saw themselves too. Their experiences can give you ideas for your own life.

Checking Your Values

Part of building a new view is knowing what you stand for. For instance, if you value honesty, then make sure you are living in line with that. If you value kindness, look for ways to show it each day. When your actions match your values, you feel more settled in who you are. This can help counter old labels that make you feel uncertain or scattered.

On the flip side, if you find yourself acting in ways that clash with your values, you might get a sense of discomfort or guilt. This does not mean you are a bad person. It may just mean your actions and your values are not lining up. Recognizing this is another part of building a true view of yourself. You can adjust your actions to be more aligned with what matters to you.

A Word About Perfection

When building a new view of yourself, some people swing to the other extreme and think they must be perfect in every way. That is not the goal. Everyone has faults. You might be great at being kind, but not so good at organizing your schedule. Or you might be skilled in math, but not as patient with people. The point is not to become perfect, but to see yourself clearly.

If you get stuck trying to be perfect, you might just create a new harsh label for yourself when you fail to reach that impossible standard. Instead, accept that you are a mix of strengths and areas you are working on. This acceptance actually helps you keep going, because you do not crumble every time you make a mistake.

An Exercise: The Future You

Imagine yourself one year from now. Think of the traits you want to develop. Write a short note to your future self, describing what you hope you have learned or done by then. This is not about wild fantasies; it is about realistic steps you can take. For example, you might write, "I hope you have finished two short stories," or "I hope you have joined a local volunteer group," or "I hope you have become more patient in stressful times."

Seal this note in an envelope or store it somewhere you can open a year later. When you read it in the future, you can see what you have done. This can remind you that you are able to make changes. Even if you do not hit every goal, noticing the progress you have made can shift your view of yourself in a positive way.

Handling Criticism While You Change

As you shift your self-view, you might run into criticism from people who are used to seeing you in the old way. Maybe you used to agree with everything they said, but now you are stating your opinions. They might push back. Here is how to handle it:

- **Stay Calm**: Getting angry or upset can make the situation worse. Take a breath and keep your voice even.
- **Explain Briefly**: If you want, you can say, "I'm trying to do things differently because I realized I had been holding myself back." You do not have to give a long explanation.
- **Stick to Your Boundaries**: If the person keeps criticizing, remind yourself that you have the right to change. You do not need their approval. It might help to step away from the conversation if it becomes too tense.

This can be hard at first, especially if the critic is someone close to you. But each time you stand up for your new view, you reinforce it in your own mind. You prove to yourself that you deserve to grow.

Telling Yourself a Better Story

Building a new view of yourself is like rewriting a story you have been telling for a long time. The difference is that now you are including facts you left out before—your strengths, your capacity to learn, and your past successes that you might have brushed aside. You are also checking where your old story might have come from, so you can see which parts do not belong to you anymore.

In the end, you will not have a perfect story. Nobody does. But you can have a more fair story, one that helps you try new things and build healthy connections. When you start to see yourself in a better light, you also begin to treat yourself more kindly. It becomes easier to let go of the past and step into new roles.

Chapter Summary

- Your view of yourself shapes your actions and overall mood.
- Old labels can come from family, friends, or personal habits.
- You can question these labels, look for times you defied them, and replace them with a more balanced view.
- Practical steps include writing a balanced self-description, asking a trusted person for honest feedback, and trying new tasks.
- Success stories, outside feedback, and skill-building activities can give you proof that you are capable of change.
- Realistic goals and daily tracking can help you see and maintain your progress.
- Shifting your self-view may cause friction with some people, but that is normal and does not mean you should stop.
- A new view does not demand perfection, only a fair sense of who you are right now and where you can grow.

Building a healthier view of yourself lays the groundwork for handling shame, which we will explore in the next chapter. Once you see that you are not defined by your past failures or labels, it becomes easier to move past shame-based thinking and step into a more open attitude toward life.

CHAPTER 4: LEARNING TO LET GO OF SHAME

Shame is a feeling that can eat away at your sense of worth. It is more than just guilt for a specific mistake. Shame is the idea that there is something wrong with you at your core. In this chapter, we will talk about how shame can form, how it affects your self-view, and ways to break free from it. By understanding shame, you can reduce its hold on your mind and feel better about yourself.

The Difference Between Shame and Guilt

It is easy to mix up shame and guilt, but they are not the same:

- **Guilt**: You feel guilt when you regret something you did. You might think, "I made a bad choice, and I want to make it right." Guilt can be useful because it points to a mistake or harm done and can push you to fix it.
- **Shame**: You feel shame when you think, "I am bad." It goes beyond a single act and targets the person as a whole. Shame can make you want to hide, because you believe you are not worthy of love or respect.

Understanding this difference matters because guilt can be managed by correcting actions, while shame often does not have a clear fix. It feels like a permanent stain on your identity rather than a mistake you can repair.

Where Does Shame Come From?

Shame can come from many sources:

1. **Family Environment**: A parent or caregiver might have used harsh words, saying things like, "You're a problem," or, "You should be

embarrassed." Over time, a child can grow up thinking they are deeply flawed.
2. **Past Trauma**: If you faced bullying or abuse, you might blame yourself. You might think, "There must be something wrong with me," even though the fault lies with the one who hurt you.
3. **Social and Cultural Rules**: Some communities have strict rules about behavior. When someone does not fit these rules, they may be made to feel shame. This can happen even if they have not done anything harmful, but simply do not follow the norm.
4. **Personal Expectations**: A person might set extremely high standards for themselves. When they cannot meet these standards, they turn that disappointment into shame, believing they are lacking in some deep way.

Shame is often built up over time. It rarely starts from one event. Instead, it grows with repeated messages that tell you, "You are not okay."

How Shame Affects You

Shame can have many effects on your life:

- **Low Self-Esteem**: If you think you are bad at the core, you might struggle to recognize any good traits you have.
- **Isolation**: Shame makes you want to hide from others. You might avoid social events or friendships because you fear people will see the "real" you.
- **Negative Self-Talk**: Shame often fuels harsh thoughts like, "I'm worthless" or "Nobody would accept me if they knew who I really am."
- **Hurtful Choices**: Some people who feel shame might seek ways to numb the pain. This can lead to harmful activities or substances to escape the feeling of not being good enough.
- **Anger**: Sometimes, shame turns into anger toward others. If you cannot bear the thought of feeling flawed, you might lash out at the slightest hint of criticism.

Recognizing these signs can help you see if shame is a factor in your life. It can also guide you toward the steps you need to heal.

Why Letting Go of Shame Is Hard

Shame can feel like a part of your identity, so it can be scary to let it go. You might wonder who you would be without that feeling. You might also worry that if you stop feeling shame, you will not have a moral compass. But letting go of shame does not mean ignoring right and wrong. You can still learn from mistakes and feel guilt when you do wrong. The big difference is that you no longer believe there is something permanently wrong with you as a person.

Another challenge is that shame can be linked to strong memories. Perhaps you remember a parent yelling at you, or a teacher humiliating you in front of the class. These memories might replay in your mind when you try to feel better about yourself. If that happens, know that these memories do not have to define you. They happened, but they do not have to shape your entire life.

Steps to Release Shame

1. **Identify the Root**: Try to figure out where your shame started. Was it a family member's constant criticism? A hurtful event in childhood? By naming the source, you can start to see that these messages came from outside of you. They might not be fair or true.
2. **Talk About It**: Shame thrives in silence. If you trust a friend, a counselor, or a support group, try talking about the things you are ashamed of. Saying them out loud often lessens their power. You might find people are more understanding than you expect.
3. **Practice Self-Compassion**: Instead of calling yourself names, speak to yourself like you would speak to a close friend. If you find this difficult, try writing a supportive note to yourself. For example, "I made a mistake, but I am still trying my best."

4. **Separate Actions from Identity**: If you did something wrong, focus on that action rather than turning it into a statement about your worth. Everyone messes up sometimes. The action can be fixed or learned from, but it does not make you a bad person.
5. **Challenge Old Beliefs**: Ask yourself: "Is it actually true that I am worthless?" Look for facts to argue against this statement. Maybe you have helped people, maybe you do well at certain tasks, or maybe you show kindness in certain areas. These facts show that the statement "worthless" is not accurate.

A Simple Exercise: Writing a "Shame Letter"

Write a letter to yourself describing why you feel shame. Include details of where the feeling came from, what triggers it, and how it makes you act. Then write a reply to that letter as if you are a kind friend. In the reply, challenge the unfair statements. Offer understanding and suggest that you do not have to be perfect to be accepted. This two-part exercise helps you see shame from a distance and gives you a chance to refute it with empathy.

Surprising Points on Shame

- **Shame Can Masquerade as Other Feelings**: Sometimes, people who feel shame get angry easily or become critical of others. They do this to avoid dealing with their own self-blame. Understanding this pattern can help you see if your anger is covering deeper shame.
- **Being Kind to Yourself Is Not Selfish**: Some people think they must be hard on themselves to be good. But kindness to yourself is a necessary step to ending shame. If you cannot be kind to yourself, you stay stuck in a cycle of self-hate, which does not help anyone.
- **Small Steps Make a Real Difference**: You do not have to fix your shame overnight. Even choosing to speak kindly to yourself once a day can start to weaken that feeling. Over time, these small steps build into a stronger sense of worth.

- **It Affects More People Than You Think**: Shame is common. Many people you admire—artists, leaders, neighbors—might be dealing with it too. Realizing shame is widespread can make you feel less alone.

Methods to Change Shame-Based Thinking

1. **Note Your Triggers**: Pay attention to times when you feel your mood drop and shame flares up. It could be at family gatherings, when looking at social media, or when facing a challenging task. Knowing these triggers allows you to prepare and use coping tools.
2. **Replace Negative Labels**: If you have certain words you call yourself—like "disgusting" or "broken"—replace them with language that points to a problem you can address, not an identity. For instance, "I messed up here, and I can do better," is different from "I'm a complete failure."
3. **Use Evidence**: If you think, "I don't deserve good things," list times you have done kind or productive actions. Even small acts, such as helping a sibling with homework or taking care of a pet, can show that you do good in the world.
4. **Mindful Awareness**: Spend a few minutes each day sitting quietly and noticing your thoughts. Try not to judge them as good or bad. Just let them come and go. This practice can help you spot shame-based thinking faster and respond in a calmer way.
5. **Seek Professional Guidance**: There are counselors and therapists who specialize in helping people with shame issues. They can guide you through methods to shift your beliefs and heal from painful past events.

Dealing with Memories that Spark Shame

Sometimes, certain memories can trigger shame. You might remember an event where you were mocked or where you felt deeply embarrassed. One technique is to bring that memory to mind, but in a safe setting—like in your room with the door closed. Imagine you as you are now, stepping into that memory. Speak to your past self with kindness. For example, "You did not deserve that," or, "You were just a child, and what happened was not your fault."

This might feel strange at first, but it can help reshape how you store that memory in your mind. Instead of letting it cause shame, you add a sense of comfort and understanding to it. Over time, the memory loses some of its power.

Social Situations and Shame

People who carry shame often struggle in social groups. They may worry about being judged or found out. Here are ways to handle that:

- **Prepare Simple Responses**: If you feel anxious about social events, have a few phrases ready. For example, if someone asks a personal question you do not want to answer, you can say something like, "I'm not comfortable talking about that right now." This helps you hold a boundary rather than feeling forced to share.
- **Pick Who You Spend Time With**: Not everyone deserves your story. Spend time with people who treat you with respect. If you are around folks who tease you or poke at your weak spots, it might be best to distance yourself.
- **Take Small Steps**: If large parties feel overwhelming, try smaller meetups or invite one or two people for a casual chat. This can help you practice being around others without feeling too exposed.
- **Give Yourself Credit**: After a social event, note any times you were able to stay present without feeling overwhelmed by shame. Even if you felt a little uneasy, the fact that you stayed and talked to people is a step forward.

Letting Go vs. Shoving Away

There is a difference between letting go of shame and trying to shove it away without dealing with it. If you shove it away, it might pop back up when something reminds you of a past hurt. Letting go means facing it, understanding where it came from, and deciding you no longer want it to define you. This process can involve tears, hard conversations, or even therapy sessions. But facing shame is the only way to truly free yourself from it.

Building a Support System

Shame can feel less heavy if you have people who accept you without judgment. This might be a friend, a sibling, a mentor, or a group at a community center. If you do not have a strong support system now, look for ways to build one. For instance, you could join a local class that interests you, volunteer for a cause, or find an online forum for people with similar interests. Genuine connections can teach you that you do not have to hide who you are.

A Daily Practice to Counter Shame

Try this each morning: stand in front of a mirror (or just sit quietly if the mirror idea feels too uncomfortable) and say a few words of kindness to yourself. It can be simple, like "I deserve to be treated with respect," or "I am allowed to make mistakes and learn." Repeat it a few times. If your mind jumps in with negative comments, gently let those thoughts pass. Do not fight them; just return to your kind words.

At first, this might seem silly or forced. But over time, it can change the way your brain talks to you. It is similar to how repeating harsh words can make you believe them—repeating kind words can reshape your beliefs too.

Examples of Letting Go of Shame

- **Apologizing and Moving On**: If your shame is tied to something you did, a sincere apology might help you feel some relief. After apologizing, allow yourself to move on, rather than staying stuck in guilt.
- **Forgiving Yourself for Past Mistakes**: We all make mistakes. Holding on to them forever and turning them into shame hurts you more than it fixes anything. Acknowledge the mistake, learn what you can, and forgive yourself as you would forgive a friend who messed up.
- **Realizing Some Things Were Not Your Fault**: If you feel shame over something that happened to you, remind yourself that being hurt by someone else is not a reflection of your worth. The responsibility for harm lies with the person who caused it.

Looking Forward

Letting go of shame does not happen in one day. It is an ongoing effort. You might wake up some mornings feeling free and confident, only to be pulled back down by a memory or a snide remark. That is okay. Each time you notice shame and choose to respond with understanding rather than self-hate, you weaken its hold.

Over the coming chapters, we will look at more ways to build a foundation of self-worth, such as setting limits with others and treating your body well. These tools will make it even easier to hold your head high and keep shame from ruling your life.

Chapter Summary

- **Shame is the belief that you are bad at your core, different from guilt over a specific act.**
- **It often comes from family, past trauma, social norms, or personal rules set too high.**

- Shame can lead to low self-esteem, isolation, anger, and unhelpful choices.
- You can let go of shame by naming where it started, talking about it, practicing kindness to yourself, and separating your actions from your self-worth.
- It helps to track when shame flares up, use mindful awareness, and seek support from caring people.
- Small steps, like self-kindness exercises and rethinking old memories, can shift deep-rooted shame.
- A support system can provide a safe space to test new ways of relating to yourself.
- Letting go of shame is about accepting yourself as a person with both good qualities and areas that need work, not about ignoring right and wrong.

With shame loosening its grip, you can begin to see your true self more clearly. This sets the stage for continuing growth in the chapters ahead. When shame no longer defines you, you open up space to learn, try new habits, and build stronger connections with others. Keep in mind that this work can be challenging, but each bit of progress matters. You are worthy of that effort.

CHAPTER 5: SELF-WORTH AND CONFIDENCE

Self-worth and confidence are closely linked to how you see yourself and how you act in the world. When your view of yourself is balanced, you recognize you have value as a person. From this sense of value, you can develop confidence in your ability to handle different tasks or challenges. This chapter will explain the differences between self-worth and confidence, why both matter, and how you can make them stronger. We will also explore some lesser-known facts about how to build these qualities in a practical way.

What Is Self-Worth?

Self-worth is the deep sense that you have value as a person, no matter what you do or what happens around you. It is not based on your grades, income, or achievements. Instead, it is the idea that you are a person who deserves basic respect and kindness. Some people call this "basic worth." Even if you fail at a task, your self-worth should not change. Even if you lose a competition or get criticized, it does not remove your basic right to be treated well.

When your self-worth is low, you might feel you are only as good as your last success or that you need to earn people's approval. But if your self-worth is healthy, you can be kind to yourself even when you fail. You understand that setbacks happen to everyone and that they do not make you a bad person.

Why Self-Worth Matters

- It helps you handle mistakes more calmly, because you do not see them as proof that you are flawed.
- It encourages better treatment from others. When you believe you deserve respect, you are more likely to speak up if someone treats you poorly.

- It helps you set fair goals. If you know you have value, you are not as desperate to chase impossible targets just to feel okay about yourself.

What Is Confidence?

Confidence is the feeling or belief that you can do something well. It is about your sense of skill or capability in specific areas. For example, you can have confidence in public speaking, cooking, or problem-solving. However, you might not have confidence in playing a sport or singing.

The important point is that confidence can change based on the skill or situation. You might be confident at work but not confident at social events. That does not mean your overall worth is any lower. It just means there is an area where you need more practice or need to learn more. True confidence is built over time by facing tasks, trying your best, and seeing your progress.

Common Mistakes About Confidence

- Some people think that being confident means never feeling nervous. In truth, even confident people can feel unsure. They just know how to keep going even when they feel anxious.
- Others assume you are born with a certain level of confidence. In fact, confidence is mostly learned. By taking on new challenges and seeing small successes, you build trust in your own abilities.

Difference Between Self-Worth and Confidence

While self-worth is about your value as a human being, confidence is about your belief in doing certain activities well. You might have strong self-worth but still lack confidence in a new skill. Or you might have moderate self-worth but feel very confident in one area where you have practiced a lot, like playing a musical instrument.

Sometimes people mix them up. They believe that if they fail at something, it lowers their value as a person. But that is not true. You can fail at a task and still remain a worthy individual. If you understand this difference, you can work on both self-worth and confidence in a healthier way. You will not feel that a slip in performance equals a loss of your personal value.

Early Clues of Low Self-Worth

1. **You Cannot Accept Praise**: When someone compliments you, do you immediately shrug it off or insist it is not true? This can be a sign you do not feel you deserve to be seen in a good light.
2. **You Feel You Must Earn Love**: If you think people only care about you because of your achievements, looks, or status, you might have a shaky sense of worth.
3. **You Apologize Too Often**: While saying sorry is polite when you have done something wrong, some people say sorry for everything, even things they cannot control. This might show you believe your presence or actions are a burden.
4. **Fear of Rejection Controls You**: A strong fear of people leaving or disliking you can point to low self-worth. You might do whatever is asked of you just to keep people around.

Early Clues of Low Confidence

1. **Avoiding New Tasks**: You might turn down new activities because you do not believe you can do them well.
2. **Overly Modest**: There is nothing wrong with being humble, but if you never admit your strengths, it might mean you do not see them.
3. **Constant Need for Approval**: You rely on others to tell you that you did okay, rather than trusting your own assessment.
4. **Negative Reaction to Failure**: When you fail, you might think, "This proves I can't do it," instead of, "I need more practice."

Building Self-Worth: Practical Methods

1. **Set a Baseline of Respect**: Tell yourself you deserve to speak up if someone treats you poorly. You do not need a special reason for that. It is just the basic respect we all deserve.
2. **Write Down Good Qualities**: Make a simple list of positive traits you have. They could be kindness, honesty, a sense of humor, or anything else. Look at this list when you feel down.
3. **Remember You Are Not Alone**: Other people make mistakes, have flaws, and feel insecure at times. Knowing that these struggles are normal can lift your sense of worth.
4. **Know Your Limits**: Having worth does not mean you can do everything. It means you recognize you are a person who can learn, grow, and also rest without seeing yourself as lesser.

Building Confidence: Practical Methods

1. **Practice, Practice, Practice**: Confidence often comes from doing something many times. If you want to be more confident in speaking in front of groups, start by speaking in front of a small, friendly group.
2. **Set Realistic Goals**: If you want to learn a new language, start with small goals like learning 10 words a week. Reaching small goals repeatedly gives you a sense of progress, which boosts confidence.
3. **Track Your Growth**: Keep a record of your improvements. If you are learning to cook, for example, note each dish you succeed in making. This evidence fights the voice in your head that says, "You can't do it."
4. **Work Through Anxiety**: You do not need to get rid of all nervousness to be confident. You can feel nervous and still take action. Over time, the nervous feeling often lessens.

Surprising Insights (Less Common Knowledge)

1. **Fake It Until You Show It**: There is an old phrase, "fake it until you make it." However, a better version is "fake it until you show it." If you stand tall, speak clearly, and behave as if you are calm, you can shift how your brain processes a stressful moment. This does not mean lying about your abilities. It means using body language and tone to help your mind feel steadier.
2. **Self-Worth Can Reduce Physical Stress**: Some research suggests that when people see themselves as worthy, their bodies have lower levels of stress hormones. This shows how mental views can influence physical states.
3. **Confidence Grows in Groups**: When you practice a skill in a group setting, you might build confidence faster because you see that other people make mistakes too. This can normalize the learning process.
4. **Mindset Over Talent**: Many studies say that believing in your ability to improve (a growth mindset) is more important for building confidence than natural talent. People who think skills can be developed usually work harder and gain more mastery.

How Self-Worth Affects Relationships

When you have a strong sense of worth, you do not rely on others to prove you are valuable. You can enjoy friendships without clinging too tightly. You can set limits if someone disrespects you. This can lead to healthier connections because you are not driven by fear or desperation.

On the other hand, if self-worth is low, you might bend over backwards to please people who do not treat you well. You might stay in situations that hurt you because you think you deserve it or you cannot do better. Over time, this can cause great harm to your mental well-being. Recognizing your own value helps you choose better friends, partners, and surroundings.

How Confidence Affects Opportunities

Confidence can open doors in many areas of life. At school or work, if you feel able to handle new tasks, you might volunteer for interesting projects. That can lead to learning experiences or even promotions. In social settings, confidence can help you start conversations or connect with people who share your interests. It does not mean you have to be the loudest or most outgoing person. Quiet confidence can also lead to strong opportunities, because people notice you are secure in who you are.

Overcoming Self-Worth Pitfalls

1. **Comparing Yourself to Others**: This is a major trap. Remember that no one has your exact combination of traits, experiences, and goals. People also tend to show only their best side in public or online, so comparing yourself to what you see can be misleading.
2. **Seeking Constant Approval**: If you find yourself fishing for compliments, ask why. Are you feeling shaky inside? Work on the cause—perhaps negative self-talk—so you do not rely on others to feel okay about yourself.
3. **All-or-Nothing Thinking**: Watch out for thoughts like, "I am either completely worthy or not worthy at all." That kind of extreme thinking does not match real life, where everyone has strengths and flaws.

Overcoming Confidence Pitfalls

1. **Overconfidence**: Sometimes people swing to the other side and claim they can do everything well, even without evidence. This can cause them to skip important steps like studying or practicing. Real confidence is honest about what you still need to learn.
2. **Tying Confidence to Ego**: Being confident is not the same as thinking you are better than others. You can be very skilled yet

remain respectful and humble toward people who are also good in their areas.
3. **Fear of Failure**: Some people think that if they fail at one task, it means they must abandon all confidence. But real confidence involves accepting that failure is part of improvement.

Techniques for Daily Life

- **Morning Reminder**: Each morning, remind yourself of one thing you value about your character (self-worth) and one skill you have improved (confidence). This trains your mind to look for positive facts about you.
- **Stay Around Positive Influences**: If certain people constantly tear you down, limit your time with them if you can. Look for people who treat you with respect, or at least neutrality, so your self-worth does not get battered.
- **Try Small Challenges**: Confidence grows when you attempt tasks that are slightly beyond your comfort level. For example, if you are learning to run, add an extra minute to your usual time. Overcoming small hurdles teaches you that you can do more than you first thought.
- **Reflect on the Day**: Before bed, quickly think of two or three things you did that showed either your sense of worth or your growing confidence. This might include saying no to something that felt unfair or speaking up in a group meeting.

A Deeper Look at Building Self-Worth

People often give advice like, "Be kind to yourself," but there are more specific ways to work on self-worth:

1. **Check Your Inner Rules**: Some people have hidden rules such as "I can only feel valuable if everyone likes me" or "I must be the best in my class to deserve respect." These rules set you up to fail because

they are impossible to meet all the time. Try rewriting these rules into kinder ones, like "I prefer when people like me, but my value does not depend on it."
2. **Visual Reminder**: Pick a short phrase that supports your worth, such as "I matter." Write it on a small card or sticky note and place it where you will see it daily. This might feel odd at first, but seeing it often can slowly change how you view yourself.
3. **Handle Mistakes with Care**: When you make a mistake, say to yourself, "I am allowed to learn from this," instead of, "I am a terrible person." Focus on what you can fix, not on labeling yourself.
4. **Stand Up for Yourself**: Practice saying things like, "Please don't speak to me that way," if someone is rude, or "I need a moment to think about that," if someone tries to rush you. Each time you stand up for yourself, you reinforce the belief that your comfort matters.

A Deeper Look at Building Confidence

Confidence is often built in layers. Here are some targeted strategies:

1. **Plan Before You Act**: If you are nervous about giving a presentation, prepare by going through it a few times at home. Organize your notes. The more prepared you feel, the more confident you will be.
2. **Get Feedback**: Ask a trusted teacher, friend, or mentor for tips. They might point out areas you can polish, which helps you improve. They can also tell you what you are already doing well, which boosts your sense of capability.
3. **Video or Audio Practice**: If you are trying to get better at speaking, record yourself. Review it to see where you look or sound confident, and which parts need adjustment. The goal is not to shame yourself but to learn.
4. **Mentally Picture Success**: Spend a few minutes picturing yourself doing a task well, whether it is singing, playing sports, or handling a job interview. This can help train your mind to believe that success is possible.

Handling Criticism in a Healthy Way

- **Self-Worth Angle**: If someone criticizes you, remind yourself that it does not reduce your value as a human being. They are talking about a specific action or result, not your entire person.
- **Confidence Angle**: Think, "Is this feedback helpful for growing my skill?" If yes, take the useful part. If not, let it go. Not all criticism is valid. Some might be from people who are upset for their own reasons.

Learning to separate your worth from criticism helps you move forward. You do not need to defend your right to exist. At the same time, you can remain open to suggestions that might help you do better.

When Self-Worth and Confidence Grow Together

A balanced sense of worth combined with growing confidence can create big changes in your life:

- **Better Stress Handling**: You feel less panicky about new tasks because you trust you can learn. You also do not believe a single failure wipes out your entire value.
- **Increased Courage to Explore**: You might try hobbies or paths that you once thought were out of reach. Even if you fail, you remain steady in knowing you have value.
- **Healthier Boundaries**: You do not let people push you into doing things that clash with your principles, because you respect yourself enough to say no.
- **More Honest Relationships**: Because you are not depending on others to feel good about yourself, you can be real with them. You can discuss problems without the fear that they will discover you are "not good enough."

Possible Obstacles and How to Address Them

1. **Deep-Rooted Self-Doubt**: If you have doubted yourself for a long time, it may take a while to shift. Be patient and keep doing small actions that show you a new way.
2. **Criticism from Close People**: Family members or friends might be used to a certain version of you. They might not want you to change. If they mock your new sense of worth or confidence, remind yourself they might feel threatened or confused. Keep going anyway.
3. **Imposter Feelings**: When you start achieving some success, you might feel you do not deserve it and that you are a fraud. This is called "imposter syndrome." It is a common feeling when you step out of your comfort zone. You can fight it by remembering all the effort you put in to reach that place.

Small Exercises You Can Try This Week

- **Self-Worth Check-In**: At the end of each day, ask yourself, "Did I show respect for my own needs today? If not, what stopped me?" This question can highlight moments where you might have ignored your worth.
- **Confidence in One Skill**: Pick one skill you want to improve. Spend 15 to 20 minutes practicing it each day. Note any small progress, such as doing a step more smoothly or making fewer mistakes.
- **Positive Talk Practice**: Choose a simple phrase like, "I can grow my skills." Say it to yourself when you notice self-doubt creeping in. This can help shift the tone of your thoughts.
- **Social Support**: Tell a supportive friend or family member about one challenge you want to tackle. Ask them to check in on you. This external support can give you a bit of extra push to stay on track.

Final Thoughts on Self-Worth and Confidence

Both of these qualities are important, but they serve different roles in your personal growth. Self-worth keeps you anchored, reminding you that you are valuable as you are. Confidence helps you take steps forward in specific tasks or areas of life.

People who mix these two ideas might feel crushed when they fail, because they treat a performance setback as a sign of losing all personal value. By separating them, you allow yourself to be human—someone who can learn, improve, and sometimes mess up—without losing basic respect for who you are.

If you ever feel stuck, remember that these traits grow with consistent practice and patient self-reflection. There will be days when you feel unsteady, and that is normal. Over time, your mind can learn a new habit of seeing yourself as worthy, and seeing your skills as something you can build step by step.

In the next chapter, we will look at setting boundaries, which is an important part of maintaining self-worth. Knowing where to draw the line with people and tasks can protect your sense of value and keep your confidence from being shaken by pressures around you.

CHAPTER 6: THE POWER OF SETTING BOUNDARIES

Boundaries are rules or limits you set to protect your well-being. They let you decide what you will accept and what you will not accept from others, as well as what you expect from yourself. Setting boundaries is not selfish. It is a healthy way to care for your mental and emotional state. When you have clear boundaries, you show self-respect and teach others how to treat you. This chapter will explain why boundaries matter, how to figure out where you need them, and how to communicate them effectively.

Why Boundaries Are Important

1. **Protection from Harm**: Without clear limits, people may take advantage of you—asking too much of your time, money, or emotional energy. Boundaries keep you safe from such overreach.
2. **Supports Self-Worth**: When you set a limit, you are telling yourself, "My comfort and well-being matter." This can strengthen your sense of worth.
3. **Makes Relationships Healthier**: People often think that being close means saying yes to everything. In reality, relationships are stronger when both sides understand each other's limits. This helps avoid resentment.
4. **Reduces Stress and Guilt**: If you do not set boundaries, you might end up overloaded with tasks or emotional burdens. Then you feel guilty or stressed. Clear boundaries can prevent that buildup.

Types of Boundaries

1. **Physical Boundaries**: Involve your personal space and body. For example, whether you are okay with hugs or need some space.

2. **Emotional Boundaries**: Involve your feelings. For instance, you might set a boundary that you will not engage in conversations that involve constant put-downs or harsh criticism.
3. **Time Boundaries**: Protect how you spend your hours. If you have a project due, you set limits on social events or phone usage so you can complete it.
4. **Material Boundaries**: Relate to your possessions or money. Maybe you do not lend out your car, or you only share certain items with close friends.
5. **Mental Boundaries**: Involve your thoughts, opinions, and right to think independently. It includes the right to disagree respectfully without being forced to adopt someone else's view.

Early Signs You Need Boundaries

- **Feeling Drained**: After spending time with certain people, do you feel exhausted or stressed? This might mean they are crossing your emotional limits.
- **Frequent Anger**: If you find yourself getting angry often, you might be letting others cross lines that you have not clearly stated.
- **Avoidance**: You might start avoiding phone calls or messages because you cannot handle another request. This can signal you need clearer rules to keep from feeling used.
- **Acting Out of Guilt**: Do you say yes just because you feel guilty saying no? Over time, this can harm your emotional health.
- **Lack of Personal Time**: If you never seem to have time for your own needs—like exercise, rest, or hobbies—you might need to set new limits on what you say yes to.

Common Barriers to Setting Boundaries

1. **Fear of Rejection**: Some people worry that if they say no, they will lose friends or upset family members.

2. **Guilt**: There is a belief that you are a bad person if you do not help everyone. While helping is kind, doing it at the cost of your health is not wise.
3. **Low Self-Worth**: If you do not think you deserve respect, you will not feel you have the right to set boundaries.
4. **Past Experiences**: Maybe you tried setting boundaries before and someone reacted badly, yelling or leaving. This can make you afraid to try again.
5. **Unclear Personal Needs**: Sometimes people do not set boundaries simply because they are not sure what they need or want.

Steps to Figure Out Your Boundaries

1. **Identify Trouble Areas**: Think of times you felt uneasy, stressed, or overwhelmed. List the situations where you wished you could say no or do less.
2. **Ask Why**: For each situation, ask yourself, "Why did I say yes, or why did I allow that behavior?" Often, the reasons are tied to fear, guilt, or habit.
3. **Decide What You Want**: If a friend calls you every night for an hour when you need to study, you might decide you want to limit calls to once or twice a week, or for a shorter time. If a coworker always gives you extra tasks, maybe you want to politely decline next time.
4. **Write It Down**: Putting your limits on paper can help you see them clearly. It also makes it easier to plan how you will communicate them to others.

Communicating Boundaries

1. **Be Brief and Clear**: You do not need a long speech. For example, say, "I can't come over today because I have other tasks I need to complete," instead of making excuses or apologizing too much.
2. **Use "I" Statements**: Such as, "I feel stressed when I have to take on extra tasks, so I need to focus on my own workload." This keeps the focus on your feelings rather than blaming the other person.

3. **Stay Calm**: If the person reacts poorly, try not to lash out in return. Remind yourself that setting a boundary is about caring for yourself, not hurting them.
4. **Repeat if Needed**: Some people might ignore your boundary at first. Continue to state your limit in a calm way. Over time, they may learn you are serious.

Handling Negative Reactions

It is possible that when you start setting boundaries, some people will not respond well. They might:

- **Argue or Guilt-Trip**: They might say things like, "You have changed," or "I thought we were friends."
- **Use Emotional Threats**: Some might threaten to leave the friendship or call you selfish.
- **Punish You**: They could withdraw their kindness, stop inviting you places, or spread negative talk about you.

While these reactions can hurt, they also reveal who respects you and who does not. If someone only values you when they can cross your limits, that might not be a healthy relationship to keep. You have the right to stand by your boundary. Over time, a true friend or a fair-minded person may adjust. Those who cannot respect you might fade out of your life, leaving space for better connections.

Surprising Insights (Less Common Knowledge)

1. **Boundaries Are Flexible, Not Rigid**: A boundary does not have to be set in stone forever. You can adjust it as your needs change. For instance, a boundary about how often you see certain people can shift if you change jobs or move.
2. **Saying No Can Improve Respect**: Sometimes, people respect you more when they see you can set limits. It shows you have self-respect, which can lead them to treat you better.

3. **Body Language Matters**: When communicating boundaries, your tone of voice and posture can affect how people receive your words. Speaking with a steady tone and standing with your head up can show you are serious.
4. **Boundary Setting Can Boost Confidence**: Each time you follow through on a boundary, you prove to yourself you can handle uncomfortable moments. This can raise your overall confidence.

Boundaries and Different Kinds of Relationships

1. **Family**: It can be tricky because families often have long-standing habits. For example, a sibling might have always borrowed money without returning it, and you might feel obligated to keep giving. Setting a limit here might feel scary, but it is possible to do so kindly yet firmly.
2. **Friends**: Good friends respect your limits. If you say you need alone time, they give you space without making you feel bad. If you notice a friend keeps pushing you, it may be time for a serious chat.
3. **Work**: You might need to limit after-hours emails or extra responsibilities if they overload you. Being clear about your availability can prevent burnout.
4. **Romantic Partners**: It is vital to communicate what is okay and what is not, whether it is how you handle shared finances, personal space, or time spent together. A healthy partnership respects both people's boundaries.
5. **Online Interactions**: In the digital age, some people might message you non-stop. You can set a boundary by deciding when you will respond or by muting notifications during personal time.

Practical Ways to Strengthen Boundaries

1. **Role-Play**: Find a friend you trust and practice saying no or setting a boundary in a pretend scenario. This helps you feel less awkward when the real moment comes.

2. **Use Technology Wisely**: If messages or calls at certain times stress you out, set your phone to "do not disturb" mode when you need quiet. This is a simple boundary with your device.
3. **Plan Ahead**: If you know a family visit or a meeting with a coworker could lead to boundary issues, plan your statements. Rehearse what you will say.
4. **Self-Check**: After a challenging interaction, ask yourself if you stayed true to your limit. If you did not, think about what stopped you and how you can handle it next time.

Boundary Myths

- **Myth 1**: Setting boundaries means you do not care about others. In truth, it is possible to be kind and helpful while still protecting your own well-being.
- **Myth 2**: Boundaries must be harsh. A boundary can be stated politely and with respect. For instance, "I appreciate your interest, but I'd rather not discuss that topic."
- **Myth 3**: If someone is upset when you set a boundary, it means you are wrong. Actually, their reaction can stem from their own expectations or insecurities. It does not automatically mean you made a mistake.
- **Myth 4**: Once a boundary is set, you never have to talk about it again. In reality, some people need reminders, and you might need to restate your limit several times.

Long-Term Effects of Setting Boundaries

- **Less Resentment**: When you set boundaries, you reduce the chances of silently building anger toward people who push you too far.
- **Greater Self-Knowledge**: Identifying and communicating your limits helps you learn more about what you need to feel healthy and balanced.

- **Improved Mental Health**: Boundaries can lower stress and prevent burnout, which benefits your mind and body.
- **A Sense of Ownership**: You feel more in control of your life because you have a say in how others treat you.

Overcoming Common Fears

1. **Fear of Being Alone**: Sometimes, people accept poor treatment because they think setting a boundary will leave them with no friends. While you might lose some connections, the ones that remain or form later will likely be more respectful.
2. **Fear of Conflict**: Saying no or disagreeing can be tense. However, gentle conflict is part of real relationships. If you always avoid it, you never fix problems.
3. **Fear of Hurting Feelings**: You can be kind while still being firm. For example, "I understand you want to hang out every weekend, but I need some personal time" respects both your needs.
4. **Fear of Change**: Any change can be uncomfortable, especially if you have always been the person who says yes. Start small, practice, and watch how it feels to stand up for yourself.

What If You Cross Someone Else's Boundary?

It is also important to respect the boundaries of others. If someone tells you they need personal space or they cannot lend money, respond calmly and politely. Apologize if needed, and try to adjust your behavior. Showing respect for another person's boundary strengthens trust. It also teaches them they can respect yours without fear of backlash.

A Useful Exercise: Boundary Mapping

1. **Make a Chart**: Divide a sheet of paper into sections for physical, emotional, time, and so on.
2. **List Current Boundaries**: Under each section, write what limits you already have. For example, "I do not answer work emails after 7 PM."
3. **List Desired Boundaries**: Add the limits you wish you had. For instance, "I want to stop lending money to relatives without clear terms."
4. **Plan a First Step**: Pick one desired boundary to work on. Write down exactly how you will communicate it. Practice if you need to.
5. **Review and Adjust**: After you try setting that boundary, note how it went. If it did not go well, think about what you can change next time.

Handling Boundaries with Close Family

Families can have strong traditions. Maybe your parents expect you to join them for every holiday or call them every day. If this feels overwhelming, it is okay to discuss making a change. Start by showing respect for the tradition while stating what you can manage. For example, "I appreciate our phone calls, but I need to limit them to once a week so I can focus on my studies."

They might react with confusion or sadness. Give them time to adjust. Stay firm in a calm way. Over time, they might see that your limit does not mean you do not love them. It simply means you are caring for your needs.

Boundaries and Personal Growth

When you set boundaries, you grow in self-awareness and self-respect. You learn what matters to you, what triggers stress, and how to protect your peace. This process can also reveal hidden strengths. For example, you might discover you are braver than you thought when you stand up for your time. Or you might find you can maintain kindness even when being firm.

This growth can feed back into building your self-worth and confidence. Once you realize you can set a boundary and survive any negative reaction, you feel more capable. This sense of capability can help in other parts of your life, like applying for jobs, starting a new hobby, or even ending toxic friendships.

Cautions

- **Do Not Use Boundaries as Threats**: A true boundary is about protecting yourself, not punishing someone else.
- **Avoid Over-Explaining**: You do not have to justify your boundary beyond stating it clearly. Over-explaining can make you seem unsure or invite more arguments.
- **Accept That Not Everyone Will Like It**: Some people prefer you remain passive. If they react poorly, that is not a sign you should give up.
- **Watch for Your Own Patterns**: Sometimes we place boundaries on others but fail to follow them ourselves. For example, demanding someone respects your time but then not respecting your own schedule.

Key Points to Remember

- **Boundaries Are Healthy**: They do not mean you are being mean or distant. They show you take your well-being seriously.
- **You Have a Right**: You are allowed to decide who has access to you, for how long, and under what conditions.
- **Be Prepared for Pushback**: Change can be uncomfortable for those who benefited from your lack of boundaries. Stand firm kindly.
- **Adjust if Needed**: As you learn and grow, you might refine your boundaries. That is normal and shows you are staying aware of your needs.

Wrapping Up This Chapter

Setting boundaries is a powerful way to protect your energy and mental health. It also supports your self-worth, because it sends the message that your needs and limits are important. Boundaries can be with friends, family, work, or even your own habits (like limiting screen time or setting a bedtime). Although it can be scary to start, many people find that once they set clear limits, they feel more stable and respected.

In the next chapters, we will explore how healthy relationships work, how to respect your body, and how to handle stress. Each of these topics links to boundaries in different ways. Whether it is saying no to unhealthy relationship patterns or setting limits on how much you push your body, boundaries will continue to play a big role. Keep practicing your new skills, and remember that each step you take in setting limits can lead to a stronger, more balanced life.

CHAPTER 7: HEALTHY RELATIONSHIPS

Healthy relationships can bring comfort, joy, and support into your life. They help you feel understood, cared for, and safe. On the other hand, a relationship filled with insults, put-downs, or manipulation can harm your self-esteem and sense of well-being. In this chapter, we will look at what makes a relationship healthy, the role of trust and communication, and how to handle conflicts in ways that do not leave lasting hurt. We will also explore what to do if a relationship turns sour and how to know if you should step away from someone who does not treat you well.

What Does a Healthy Relationship Look Like?

A healthy relationship is one in which both people feel respected and able to be themselves without fear. This applies to friendships, romantic partnerships, family relationships, and even the way you relate to coworkers or classmates. Each type of relationship can have different rules and dynamics, but certain features signal that it is likely to be healthy:

1. **Respect**: Both individuals treat each other with kindness. They do not call each other names or belittle each other's opinions.
2. **Honesty**: Each person can speak openly about thoughts and feelings without hiding the truth to avoid arguments. There is no constant lying or sneaking around.
3. **Equality**: Neither person dominates the other. Decisions are shared, and each person's needs are considered.
4. **Safe Communication**: You can share worries, sadness, or mistakes without fear that the other will use your words against you.
5. **Personal Space**: Healthy relationships allow for separate hobbies, friends, or personal time. You do not have to spend every moment together.
6. **Support**: When one person faces a problem, the other offers help in a way that encourages growth, rather than making the person feel incapable or weak.

Understanding Red Flags vs. Positive Signs

Sometimes it can be tough to tell if a relationship is truly healthy, especially if you have grown up around unhealthy patterns. Here are a few red flags—warning signs that might signal trouble:

- **Name-Calling or Frequent Insults**: Even if said in a "joking" way, repeated put-downs can harm self-esteem and show a lack of respect.
- **Control and Manipulation**: One person tries to limit the other's contact with friends or family. Or they manipulate situations to get their own way.
- **Threats**: If disagreements often come with threats to leave, harm, or make life difficult, it indicates a problem.
- **Lack of Trust**: Constant spying on or checking up on the other, not because there was a betrayal in the past, but as a routine act. This shows an absence of healthy trust.

Positive signs are the opposite: praising each other, supporting each other's personal goals, and not trying to make the other feel guilty for having outside interests. Keep an eye on how each person treats the other on both good days and bad days. A healthy bond will show respect even when there is a disagreement.

The Role of Communication

Communication is the basis of any healthy relationship. It is how you share your ideas, feelings, and concerns. Here are ways to keep communication clear:

1. **Active Listening**: This means giving the speaker your full attention. Put aside your phone, maintain comfortable eye contact, and show that you are hearing them. When you respond, restate a part of what they said to ensure you understand correctly.

2. **Speak Clearly**: Instead of hinting at your feelings, say them plainly in a calm tone. For example, "I feel worried when you do not text me back for days," is clearer than, "You never care about me!"
3. **Avoid Accusations**: Use "I" statements. For instance, "I feel upset when I am shouted at," instead of, "You are always mean!" This approach keeps the focus on the behavior rather than attacking the person.
4. **Pick the Right Time**: If you need to discuss a sensitive issue, try not to start the conversation when either person is very angry, tired, or in a rush. Scheduling a calm moment can make a big difference.

Building and Keeping Trust

Trust is built over time. In any close connection, small daily actions can either strengthen or weaken trust. Simple acts like being on time, keeping promises, and avoiding secretive behavior help create a solid foundation. If trust is broken, rebuilding it involves honest talks, taking responsibility for the harm done, and showing through actions—not just words—that the wrongdoing will not happen again.

- **Follow Through on Promises**: If you say you will call someone at a specific time or meet them somewhere, do so unless there is a real emergency. Doing what you say you will do shows you can be counted on.
- **Be Real**: If you act one way in person but another way behind someone's back, it can cause suspicion. Treat people with consistent respect, whether they are present or not.
- **Allow Second Chances Carefully**: If someone has broken trust, it can be given again if you see real change. But watch out for repeated patterns. If they keep doing the same thing, you may need to consider if the relationship is right for you.

Respecting Personal Boundaries

Boundaries protect each person's sense of comfort and well-being within a relationship. Sometimes, people assume that being close means you share everything or spend every second together. However, a respectful bond allows each person to say no, ask for personal time, or refuse to do things that make them uncomfortable.

For example, you might have a rule that you need one hour alone every evening to recharge your mind. A healthy friend or partner will honor that rule without complaining that you are neglecting them. Chapter 6 went into detail about setting boundaries. When both people recognize and respect boundaries, it reduces frustration and fights.

Handling Conflict Without Causing Lasting Harm

Disagreements happen in all relationships. Two people will not always see things the same way. Conflict, by itself, is not a sign of an unhealthy bond. What matters is how you handle it:

1. **Stay Calm**: If you feel your anger rising, take a moment to breathe. Count to ten or ask for a short break. It is better to pause than to say something you will regret.
2. **Focus on the Issue**: Keep the discussion about the specific problem, not about the other person's character. Instead of, "You are always lazy," try, "I am upset because I feel I am the only one who cleans the kitchen."
3. **Look for Solutions**: Aiming to "win" an argument can damage trust. Instead, look for a compromise. Ask, "What can we do so both of us feel better about this?"
4. **Apologize Sincerely**: If you say or do something hurtful, admit it. A real apology includes showing you regret your actions and plan to change them in the future.

When a Relationship Turns Unhealthy

Sometimes, despite your best efforts, a relationship remains filled with negativity or even emotional or physical harm. If you notice these signs, you may be in an unhealthy situation:

- **You Are Afraid to Speak Your Mind**: You worry that sharing a simple opinion will lead to anger or mocking.
- **You Feel Less About Yourself**: The relationship tears you down, making you doubt your worth.
- **Guilt Is Used as a Weapon**: The other person constantly makes you feel guilty to get their way.
- **Threats or Fear**: The other person threatens you or those you care about, or you fear what they might do if you end things.

In such cases, stepping away or seeking help from a counselor or support line is often necessary. If the situation involves any form of abuse, do not wait to reach out for professional advice or help from a trusted friend, teacher, or authority figure.

Growing Together

A healthy relationship should not trap you. It should allow you and the other person to grow. This means being supportive when someone wants to learn a new skill or take up a new interest. It also means celebrating each other's successes without envy or mockery. Having someone cheer for your progress can boost your self-confidence and sense of worth.

However, if one person tries to hold the other back—saying things like, "You can't do that," or "You should just stay in your lane"—that can limit personal growth. Mutual respect includes cheering on new goals and understanding that both people can learn new things and change over time.

Balancing Needs and Wants

In any bond, there are two sets of needs: yours and the other person's. Balancing them involves:

- **Listening**: Take time to hear what the other person needs. Maybe your friend needs space to study and can only meet on weekends.
- **Expressing**: Share your needs as well. If you want more communication or help with something, say so.
- **Finding Middle Ground**: Try to figure out ways that respect both sides. This can be small, like agreeing on which movie to watch, or large, like deciding where to live in the future.

This process can be tricky, especially if both people want different things. But with calm communication, it is possible to find solutions or compromises. If a middle ground cannot be found, sometimes it means the relationship is not a good match.

Different Types of Relationships

1. **Friendships**: Friends are people you share hobbies, interests, or experiences with. True friends are there for each other but also allow independence.
2. **Family Bonds**: You might share history and strong ties. Family relationships can be supportive or strained, depending on how members treat each other.
3. **Romantic Partnerships**: Trust, respect, and good communication are key here. A romantic connection should not be a source of constant stress, fear, or jealousy.
4. **Professional Relationships**: You might have to work closely with colleagues or managers. Even though these are not typically personal, respect and fairness still matter.

Knowing how to handle each type of relationship can help you navigate life. The core elements—respect, honesty, and healthy boundaries—remain important across all of them.

Handling Differences and Diversity

In today's world, people come from different backgrounds, cultures, or beliefs. You and someone else might have different traditions or perspectives. A healthy connection recognizes those differences without forcing one person to change who they are. You do not have to agree on everything, but you can learn to respect each other's views. If the differences are so big that you cannot find any common ground, you might limit the topics you discuss, or you may decide the relationship does not work.

Jealousy and Envy

Jealousy can pop up in friendships or romantic bonds. It often comes from fear of losing someone or feeling less important. If you feel jealous, try to see what is causing it. Are you worried that your friend likes someone else more than you? Are you afraid your partner will leave you? Talking calmly about these worries can help clear the air. Healthy relationships include honesty about jealous feelings without blaming or accusing the other person.

Envy, on the other hand, is when you feel bitter about someone else's achievements or blessings. This can cause hidden anger or resentment. If you notice envy, remind yourself that someone else's success does not take away from your worth. Support them, and look for ways to improve your own goals rather than viewing theirs as a threat.

Forgiveness and Moving On

At times, people will let you down. Maybe a friend breaks a promise or a sibling says something hurtful. Learning to forgive is part of keeping relationships alive. Forgiveness does not mean you pretend the hurt never happened. It means you choose not to hold it against the other person forever. You allow room for healing and, if possible, rebuilding trust.

However, if the person keeps hurting you without any sign of change, forgiveness might mean letting go of anger while still protecting yourself by stepping away.

Surprising Insights About Healthy Relationships

1. **Healthy Conflict Can Strengthen Bonds**: Avoiding conflict at all costs might seem peaceful, but it can lead to unspoken issues that build resentment. Carefully managed conflict can clear the air.
2. **Quality Matters More Than Quantity**: Having one close, understanding friend can be more fulfilling than having many acquaintances. Depth in a relationship often brings more support than having a large circle where no one truly knows you.
3. **Personal Responsibility**: In a healthy bond, each person takes responsibility for their own emotions and actions. You can ask for help, but you do not blame the other person if you are unhappy. You look at your own choices too.
4. **Changing Roles Over Time**: A friend from childhood might serve a certain role in your life, but as you both mature, the relationship might shift. This can be normal. Some friendships adapt and remain close, while others fade. Change does not mean you failed; it can mean you have grown in different directions.

Practical Steps to Strengthen Your Relationships

- **Give Genuine Praise**: Let people know when you appreciate something they have done. Small compliments—"I like how you handled that situation" or "You did great on your presentation"—can make them feel valued.
- **Say "Thank You" Often**: Gratitude can soften conflicts and build warmth. When someone does something nice, no matter how small, thank them.
- **Accept Help**: If a friend or partner offers help, do not push them away out of pride. Working together can deepen your connection.

- **Set Shared Goals**: Whether it is planning a trip or saving money, having shared goals with someone can bring a sense of teamwork.
- **Give Space**: Make sure you both have time to yourselves. Spending every moment together can lead to friction and loss of individual identity.
- **Check in Regularly**: Simple messages like, "How are you today?" or a quick call can keep the connection strong, especially if you do not see each other daily.

Knowing When to End or Reduce Contact

Ending a bond can be a painful decision, but sometimes it is the right one. You may choose to part ways with someone who repeatedly disrespects you, ignores your boundaries, or causes you harm. If the relationship drains you more than it lifts you, it might be time to step back. Before making a final decision, you can try to discuss the issues. If nothing changes and you still feel hurt or unsafe, it is usually best to distance yourself.

In some cases, you might not want to end the relationship fully, but you reduce your contact or shift how you interact. This can apply to family members you cannot cut out of your life entirely, but you can decide to limit how often you meet or how much personal information you share.

Moving Forward with Healthier Bonds

Healthy relationships are not perfect, but they feel balanced and respectful most of the time. They help you learn more about yourself and the other person. They also teach you how to solve conflicts without resorting to hurtful language or actions. Over time, nurturing these bonds can boost your sense of security and self-worth.

Remember, you deserve relationships that treat you well. By applying clear communication, mutual respect, and healthy boundaries, you can build stronger connections. At the same time, you can step away from those who harm your well-being. This approach will support the personal growth you are aiming for in this book.

Chapter Summary

- Healthy relationships are built on respect, honesty, and safe communication.
- Red flags include name-calling, threats, or controlling behavior.
- Trust grows through consistent actions like keeping promises and showing genuine care.
- Boundaries protect personal comfort; a healthy partner or friend honors them.
- Conflict is normal, but it should be handled with calm communication and a focus on finding solutions.
- Signs of an unhealthy bond include fear, constant guilt, and feeling worse about yourself.
- When a relationship has constant negativity, it may be time to seek help or step away.
- Knowing when to forgive and when to let go can keep you from staying in a harmful situation.
- Practical steps such as offering thanks, giving space, and checking in regularly help make connections stronger.
- Sometimes ending or reducing contact is the wisest choice for your mental well-being.

As you continue, keep an eye on how people in your life treat you and how you respond to them. Strive for bonds that support who you are and encourage your growth. In the next chapter, we will turn our attention to caring for your body, recognizing that a healthy mind often thrives alongside a healthy body.

CHAPTER 8: RESPECT FOR YOUR BODY

Your mind and your body are connected. When you treat your body kindly, it can help your mood, energy, and overall sense of worth. But in a world filled with unrealistic images of beauty and quick-fix diets, many people lose sight of what it really means to respect their own bodies. This chapter explores ways to care for your physical self in a balanced manner, how to recognize signs of neglect, and why body respect is an important part of liking who you are.

The Link Between Body and Mind

If you have ever felt groggy after staying up too late or grumpy when you skipped a meal, you have experienced the effect of your physical state on your mood. When your body is run-down, your thoughts can become more negative. On the flip side, when you are well-rested and well-fed, you often handle stress better. Caring for your physical health is not just about looking a certain way; it is about supporting your emotional and mental well-being.

Signs You Are Not Respecting Your Body

1. **Skipping Meals or Overeating Constantly**: Ignoring your body's signals about hunger and fullness can lead to low energy and guilt.
2. **Never Getting Enough Sleep**: Chronic tiredness can harm your mood, concentration, and overall health.
3. **Pushing Through Pain**: While slight discomfort in exercise might be normal, real pain can mean injury or stress. Ignoring pain signals can lead to lasting damage.
4. **Harsh Self-Talk About Appearance**: Calling yourself mean names or constantly focusing on body flaws is a sign of self-disrespect.
5. **Lack of Movement**: Sitting all day without any form of physical activity can lower your energy and affect the balance of hormones that keep you feeling stable.

What Does It Mean to Respect Your Body?

Respecting your body means recognizing that it is the physical vessel through which you experience life. It is not about having the "perfect" figure or fitting a specific beauty standard. Instead, it involves:

- **Listening to Signals**: Eating when you are hungry, resting when you are tired, and paying attention to pain or discomfort.
- **Offering Proper Nourishment**: Trying to include a balance of foods that give you the nutrients you need, while still enjoying treats in moderation.
- **Staying Active**: Engaging in some form of physical movement that you find enjoyable and sustainable.
- **Avoiding Harmful Habits**: This includes trying not to overdo it with junk food, or avoiding misuse of substances like drugs or alcohol.
- **Accepting Your Unique Shape**: Bodies come in different forms. Treating yours with kindness, rather than scorn, can help your mental state.

Moving Away from Negative Body Thoughts

It is common to have thoughts like, "I am too fat," "I am too thin," or "My nose is weird." But if these thoughts become constant and harsh, they can chip away at your self-esteem. Here are some ways to move away from such negativity:

1. **Watch Your Inner Comments**: Become aware of when you call yourself negative names or compare yourself harshly to others. Awareness is the first step to changing these thoughts.
2. **Question Unrealistic Standards**: Magazines, social media, or movies often show bodies that have been heavily edited or belong to people whose job is to maintain a certain look. Remind yourself that real life bodies are more varied.

3. **Compliment Your Body's Function**: Instead of focusing on shape, think about what your body can do—walk, dance, hug, laugh. Let yourself feel some gratitude for these abilities.
4. **Stop Comparing**: Everyone has different genetics, lifestyles, and challenges. Comparing your body to someone else's is like comparing apples and oranges. Focus on your own progress and well-being.

Balanced Eating Without Judgment

Eating can be a source of stress if you feel guilty about every bite or if you swing between extreme dieting and overeating. Balanced eating means:

- **Regular Meals**: Try to have a routine that includes breakfast, lunch, and dinner. Add small snacks if needed.
- **Variety**: Aim to include different food groups—proteins, carbs, healthy fats, vegetables, fruits—so that your body gets what it needs.
- **Permission to Enjoy**: Treats are not evil. A piece of dessert or a favorite snack in moderation can be part of a balanced approach.
- **Mindful Eating**: Pay attention while you eat. Notice flavors, textures, and when you start feeling full. Avoid scrolling on your phone or watching TV during every meal. This awareness can help you avoid overeating and increase satisfaction.

Movement That Suits You

Not everyone likes the same form of exercise. Some people love running; others prefer yoga, dancing, or swimming. The best form of physical activity is the one you can enjoy and keep doing regularly. Movement benefits your body by improving blood flow, muscle strength, and even mood. When you move, your brain releases chemicals that can help you feel more positive.

- **Start Small**: If exercise is new to you, begin with a short walk or easy stretches. Increase the intensity or length bit by bit.

- **Pick Something Fun**: If you hate running, do not force yourself to run every day. Try a dance class, a biking path, or even a home workout video you enjoy.
- **Listen to Your Limits**: A little push is good, but if you are out of breath to the point of feeling ill or experiencing sharp pain, slow down or stop.

Getting Enough Rest

Sleep is often overlooked, but it is crucial for body respect. When you sleep, your body repairs itself, your brain processes information, and you regain the energy to face a new day.

- **Set a Bedtime**: Choose a consistent time to go to bed. Turning off screens at least 30 minutes before sleeping can help.
- **Create a Calming Routine**: A warm shower, reading a paper book, or listening to soft music can help signal your body that it is time to rest.
- **Avoid Heavy Meals Right Before Bed**: Eating a huge meal or very spicy food late at night can disrupt your sleep. Try to space dinner a bit earlier if possible.

Handling External Pressures

Often, friends, family, or popular culture put pressure on how we should look or what size we should be. You might hear comments like, "You need to lose weight," or "You are looking too thin." While some comments are made with concern, others can be hurtful or misguided. Respecting your body means deciding what goals and practices are right for you, not just following someone else's idea of what you should be.

If you feel someone is constantly judging your appearance, you can set a boundary, such as: "I would prefer not to discuss my weight or body shape." You can also remember that any changes you choose to make should come from your own desire to be healthier, not from shame or fear of judgment.

Overcoming Shame Linked to Body Image

Some people feel shame about their bodies, especially if they do not fit certain social ideals. This shame can lead to hiding, avoiding activities like swimming because you do not want to be seen in a swimsuit, or even avoiding social gatherings. Overcoming this shame is similar to letting go of the more general shame discussed in Chapter 4:

1. **Identify the Source**: Is it comments from childhood, media images, or a specific event where you were teased?
2. **Challenge the Message**: Ask yourself if it is truly fair to say your worth depends on fitting a certain size or shape. Most often, these messages are narrow and do not consider the wide range of healthy bodies.
3. **Find Role Models of Different Body Types**: Seeing people who look more like you can help remind you that your body is not "wrong." There are athletes of all sizes, for instance, proving that ability does not always match a single body image.
4. **Consider Professional Help**: If body shame becomes severe—leading to disordered eating or constant self-hate—talk to a counselor or mental health professional.

Practical Body Respect Habits

1. **Stretch or Move in the Morning**: A quick set of stretches after you wake up helps you connect with your body in a positive way.
2. **Stay Hydrated**: Water is vital for many body functions. Keep a water bottle handy, especially if you are active or live in a hot climate.
3. **Avoid Excessive Comparison**: Social media is full of images that may not show the reality of someone's life. Focus on your own progress and health markers, like your energy level.
4. **Dress Comfortably**: Wear clothes that fit well and make you feel good. Squeezing into outfits that hurt or always wearing baggy

clothes to hide might come from body dissatisfaction. Find styles that suit you and let you move freely.

Surprising Points About Body Respect

- **Mental Images Matter**: Some research suggests visualizing yourself engaging in healthy habits can increase the odds of doing them. For example, picturing yourself enjoying a walk can make you more likely to actually do it.
- **Posture Influence**: Standing or sitting up straight can change your mood and energy levels. Slouching might make you feel more tired or negative, while upright posture can boost self-confidence.
- **Sunlight and Fresh Air**: Spending time outside can help improve mood, vitamin D levels, and overall well-being. Even a short walk in daylight can be uplifting.
- **Breathing Techniques**: Taking slow, deep breaths can lower stress. Sometimes just a few calm breaths can center you if you feel tense about your body or anything else.

Avoiding Extremes

In trying to respect your body, watch out for extremes. Going from never exercising to working out two hours a day, or from eating junk food daily to cutting out entire food groups overnight, can be stressful and lead to burnout. A balanced, gradual shift is more likely to last. If you ever feel you are taking a habit to an unhealthy extreme—such as measuring every calorie or pushing exercise until you are constantly exhausted—take a step back. It might be time to talk to a professional for guidance.

Facing Physical Challenges or Illness

Some people have physical conditions or disabilities that limit what they can do. Respecting your body in those situations might mean working closely with healthcare providers, doing specialized exercises, or using assistive devices. If you have a chronic condition, it is still possible to have a respectful attitude toward your body by focusing on what you can do rather than only on what you cannot.

For example, if you are on crutches, maybe you can do seated exercises to keep some muscles active. If you have certain dietary restrictions, look for creative recipes that fit your health needs without becoming bland. In every case, the focus should be on realistic well-being, not chasing impossible ideals.

Understanding That Bodies Change

Throughout life, bodies change naturally. Children grow into teens, teens into adults, and so on. Metabolism and hormones fluctuate. Pregnancy, aging, injuries, and illnesses can alter your shape or your abilities. Respecting your body also means adapting to these changes rather than fighting them. While you can make healthy lifestyle choices, you cannot always control the aging process or other shifts. Accepting that change is part of being alive can help you find more peace with your physical self.

Body Respect and Self-Worth

Since this book focuses on liking yourself, remember that your body is part of who you are—but it does not define your entire identity. You can work on improving your health or fitness while still recognizing that your worth is not tied to having a certain kind of body. A balanced view is: "I want to take care of this body so I can feel better and do more, but my value as a person does not rise or fall with each pound or clothing size."

When you show your body kindness—through proper rest, decent nutrition, enjoyable movement—you are sending a message to yourself that you matter. This can reinforce other parts of your self-improvement journey, such as mental health and emotional balance. Likewise, if you constantly punish your body or speak poorly of it, that can create stress and sadness, making it harder to maintain a positive sense of who you are.

Simple Routines to Try

- **Daily Check-In**: Each morning or evening, ask yourself if you have moved enough, eaten balanced meals, and rested properly. If not, plan a small adjustment.
- **Mindful Meal Once a Day**: Pick one meal to eat without any distractions. Notice the flavors, chew slowly, and see if it affects how much you enjoy and how full you feel.
- **Short Exercise Breaks**: If you work at a computer or study for long hours, take a 5-minute stretch or walk break each hour. This helps blood flow and keeps energy more stable.
- **Body Appreciation Notes**: Once a week, write something you appreciate about your body (e.g., "My legs helped me walk around the park today," or "My hands allow me to write and draw").

Dealing with Setbacks

You might set a goal to walk three times a week or eat more veggies, but then life gets busy, or you lose motivation. It is okay to fall off track. Instead of feeling like a failure, see it as a chance to learn. Ask yourself what got in the way. Maybe you need to adjust your plan to something more realistic. Or maybe you need a partner to join you so you both keep each other motivated.

If you catch yourself returning to negative body talk or pushing yourself in unhealthy ways, recognize that you can course-correct. Look at what triggered the setback, address it calmly, and pick up where you left off.

Sharing Your Body Respect Journey with Others

If you live with family or have friends who also struggle with body image, you might suggest group activities that support respectful habits. For instance, cooking a healthy meal together can be a fun way to practice balanced eating, or going for a group walk can turn movement into a social event. Sharing your thoughts about body respect can also help you stay focused, since discussing a goal often makes it feel more real.

Be cautious, though, with people who might push extreme diets or make critical remarks. You can respectfully decline to follow their advice if it does not align with your balanced approach. Setting boundaries around body talk, such as, "I prefer not to discuss crash diets," can protect your mindset.

Chapter Summary

- Your body and mind influence each other; taking care of one supports the other.
- Respecting your body involves balanced eating, regular movement, proper rest, and kind self-talk.
- Neglect may show up in skipping meals, lack of sleep, ignoring pain, or constant self-criticism.
- Choose exercise routines you enjoy and can stick with, rather than forcing yourself into something you hate.
- Sleep routines are key for mental and physical recovery; turn off screens and create a calm setting to improve rest.
- External pressures about beauty or size can harm self-esteem. Set boundaries with people who comment too much on your body.
- Body shame is common but can be challenged by identifying its source, questioning unrealistic standards, and seeking diverse role models.
- Avoid extreme dieting or exercise plans. Seek balance and gradual improvement.

- Your body changes over time due to growth, aging, or health issues. Respect means adapting rather than fighting these changes.
- Practical steps like mindful eating, short exercise breaks, and daily check-ins can boost body respect.
- Setbacks happen; use them to learn and adjust rather than quitting or blaming yourself.
- Sharing your goals with supportive friends or family can help, but guard against negative or extreme influences.

Your body is your constant companion. By treating it with thoughtfulness, you reinforce the message that you are a person of worth. As you move on, keep these tips in mind to nourish both your body and spirit. In the following chapters, we will look at more strategies—like handling stress and anxiety, setting realistic goals, and learning from mistakes—that will combine to give you a stronger sense of self.

CHAPTER 9: MANAGING STRESS AND WORRY

Stress is a normal part of life. At times, we feel a sense of pressure or fear when deadlines approach, when there is a big change, or when we are uncertain about the future. Worry can also creep into our minds and affect how we see ourselves and the world. If stress and worry build up, they can affect sleep, mood, and even relationships. In this chapter, we will talk about why stress happens, how worry develops, and ways to deal with them. By the end, you should have some practical methods to lessen stress and handle worry so it does not take over your life.

What Causes Stress?

Stress can come from many places. Some people feel tense because of school or work. Others might feel under strain because of money problems, family conflicts, or health concerns. Even positive events—like starting a new job or moving to a better home—can create stress because there is a sense of the unknown.

Common causes include:

1. **Too Many Tasks**: Having more to do than you can manage (like a huge to-do list that never ends).
2. **Big Changes**: Life changes (like changing schools, moving cities, or having a child) can create emotional strain.
3. **Fear of Failing**: Worrying about not doing well enough at work, in school, or in personal goals.
4. **Relationship Troubles**: Arguments with friends, family, or romantic partners can increase stress levels.
5. **Uncertain Future**: Not knowing what will happen with your job, health, or relationships can make your mind race with worry.

When stress goes on for a long time, it can lead to deeper problems like sleeplessness, muscle pain, or ongoing anxiety.

Why Worry Feels So Strong

Worry is the mind's way of trying to handle potential threats or problems. Our brains are wired to notice danger so we can stay safe. In older times, people had to watch out for animals or threats in the wild. Today, our threats are often not physical but emotional—like fear of losing a job or not being liked by peers. The mind still reacts strongly, leading to racing thoughts or constant concern.

When we worry, we often think about "what if" scenarios. For example:

- "What if I fail the exam?"
- "What if I never find a job?"
- "What if people think I'm not good enough?"

These thoughts can cycle in the mind, feeding anxiety. Over time, we might build the habit of worrying about small things. This can drain our energy and make us feel tense all the time.

The Cost of Constant Stress and Worry

1. **Physical Problems**: Stress can cause headaches, stomach issues, and lowered immune function. You might notice you get sick more easily.
2. **Emotional Drain**: Constant stress can lead to sadness or loss of motivation. Overly worried people might struggle to enjoy normal activities because they are always on edge.
3. **Trouble Sleeping**: Racing thoughts can make it hard to fall asleep or stay asleep. Lack of rest then adds to daily stress.
4. **Strained Relationships**: If you are tense or irritable, friends or family might find it tough to connect with you. You might snap at people without meaning to.
5. **Reduced Focus**: Worry can fill your mind, leaving little room for creativity or clear thought.

All of this can lead to an ongoing cycle: worry leads to less rest and more tension, which leads to more worry, and so on.

Recognizing Early Signs

Learning to notice the early signs of stress or worry can help you act before things get worse:

- **Racing Heart**: You might feel your heartbeat speeding up when you think about certain problems.
- **Tense Muscles**: Many people store tension in their shoulders, neck, or jaw.
- **Overthinking**: You catch yourself going over the same thought again and again.
- **Irritability**: You get annoyed by small things that normally would not bother you.
- **Change in Appetite**: Some people eat more when stressed, while others lose their appetite.

When you see these signs, it is like a small alarm telling you it might be time to pause, take a breath, and use methods to reduce stress.

Methods to Ease Stress in Daily Life

1. **Break Tasks into Steps**
   A large project or a long to-do list can feel impossible. Instead, break them into small actions. Focus on one step at a time, rather than the entire project at once. For example, if you have to write a report, you might start with just one section or gather references on the first day.
2. **Use Time Blocks**
   Instead of trying to do everything at once, set short blocks of time (like 25 minutes) to focus on a single task, followed by a quick break. This approach (often called the "Pomodoro technique") can help you stay productive without feeling overwhelmed.
3. **Practice Relaxation**
   Activities like slow breathing, gentle stretching, or a warm bath can calm the mind. Even a quick break where you close your eyes and breathe deeply for a minute can lower tension.

4. **Spend Time on Something You Enjoy**
   Hobbies can reduce stress by allowing you to focus on pleasant activities. It could be painting, reading, playing a musical instrument, or even chatting with a friend. The key is to choose something that naturally helps you feel relaxed.
5. **Physical Exercise**
   Movement can release chemicals in the brain that help you feel calmer and happier. A simple walk, short bike ride, or some easy at-home exercises can do wonders.

Ways to Stop Worry in Its Tracks

1. **Question the Worry**
   Ask yourself, "Is this worry based on fact, or am I imagining the worst?" Often, we overestimate bad outcomes. Checking reality can ease the fear.
2. **Limit "What If" Thoughts**
   If you find yourself stuck in "what if" mode, try writing down the worst-case scenario, the best-case scenario, and the most likely scenario. Seeing it on paper may help you see that the worst-case outcome is not as likely as you fear.
3. **Schedule Worry Time**
   This might sound strange, but some people find it helpful to set aside a small block of time each day—maybe 10 or 15 minutes—just to let themselves worry. If a worry pops up at another time, remind yourself you will handle it in your "worry time." This can prevent worry from taking over the entire day.
4. **Replace Worry with Action**
   If something is bothering you (like an upcoming test), see if there is a small step you can take to prepare (like reviewing a chapter or practicing a few test questions). Turning worry into action can give you a sense of control.
5. **Use a Thought-Stopping Word**
   Some people pick a word like "stop" and say it softly (or in their head) when worry thoughts arise. After saying it, they shift to a different activity or thought. This can break the worry cycle.

Surprising Tips for Stress and Worry

1. **Grounding Through Senses**
   When you feel overwhelmed, try focusing on your senses for a moment. Name five things you can see, four things you can touch, three you can hear, two you can smell, and one you can taste. This can bring your attention back to the present and slow worry.
2. **Handwriting Notes**
   Writing by hand (instead of typing) about your stress or worry can have a calming effect. The act of physically moving a pen across paper is slower than typing, which can help you process thoughts more gently.
3. **Progressive Relaxation**
   Tense and then relax each muscle group in your body, one at a time. Start with your toes, then your feet, then your calves, and so on, up to your face. This helps your body release stored tension.
4. **Soothing Smells**
   Some scents can calm the mind. Examples include mild lavender or chamomile. You can use a small candle or essential oil diffuser if it helps. While not a cure for stress, a gentle scent can soothe nerves in certain people.

Handling Stressful Events in Real Time

Sometimes stress hits you at a specific moment—like just before a speech or an important meeting. Having a quick method ready can help:

- **Take a Quick Break**: If possible, excuse yourself to the restroom or a quiet corner. Take a few slow, deep breaths.
- **Positive Self-Talk**: Remind yourself you have prepared for this moment, or that you can handle the first step. If a negative thought arises, replace it with a more balanced one.
- **Stay in the Present**: Rather than thinking, "What if I mess up?" focus on the immediate actions you need to take, like looking at your notes or greeting people calmly.

Turning Stress into a Helpful Signal

A small amount of stress can actually be useful. It can prompt you to study for a test or to prepare well for a job interview. The key is finding that balance between helpful stress and overwhelming stress. If you can learn to see mild stress as a sign that you care about something, you may be able to turn it into energy for positive action. But once stress becomes too big or never-ending, it stops being helpful and starts harming you.

Tips for Ongoing Stress Management

1. **Keep a Stress Journal**
   Write down the times you feel most tense, what happened, and how you responded. Over time, you might see a pattern. Maybe certain people or places trigger stress. Knowing the pattern helps you plan ahead or adjust how you handle those situations.
2. **Seek Support**
   Talk to a trusted friend, family member, or counselor. Sometimes just talking about worries can reduce their weight. You do not have to face stress alone.
3. **Review Your Priorities**
   If your schedule is jam-packed, see if there is anything you can cut back on. Saying no to extra tasks or commitments can protect you from constant overload.
4. **Practice Gratitude**
   Spending a moment each day to note a few things you appreciate can shift your focus away from stress. It does not erase problems, but it helps balance your thinking.
5. **Plan for Breaks**
   If you know a busy week is coming, plan small rewards or breaks for yourself. This could be as simple as 15 minutes of quiet time or enjoying a favorite snack once you finish a task.

Worry vs. Problem Solving

Worry can feel like you are trying to solve problems, but often it is just running the same scary thoughts on repeat. True problem solving involves identifying the issue and brainstorming realistic steps to address it. Ask these questions:

- **What is the exact problem I'm facing?**
- **What are some possible solutions or steps I can take?**
- **Who can I ask for advice or help?**
- **When can I start taking action?**

Writing these down can shift your mind from worry to purposeful thinking. Even if you do not find a perfect solution, the act of looking for answers can make you feel less stuck.

Working with Professionals

If stress or worry has become too big to manage alone, do not hesitate to seek professional help. A counselor, therapist, or mental health professional can teach you methods that are specific to your situation. They might show you how to reframe negative thoughts or guide you through relaxation exercises. These experts are trained to help people handle intense stress and anxiety in a way that fits their life and personal challenges.

Stress-Busting Activities

1. **Creative Outlets**: Drawing, coloring, or writing in a journal can calm your mind. The point is not to produce a masterpiece, but to let your thoughts flow out in a gentle way.
2. **Music**: Listening to songs you enjoy or playing an instrument can release tension. Some people find that upbeat tunes lift their mood, while soft melodies help them relax.
3. **Nature Time**: If possible, spend a few moments in a park or any green area. Fresh air, plants, and a change of scenery can lower stress levels.

4. **Laughter**: Watch a funny show, read a comic, or recall something silly that happened recently. Laughter can ease physical tension and help you gain a fresh outlook.

Long-Term Lifestyle Factors

While quick fixes help in the moment, consider your overall habits too. Here are some lifestyle tips that support lower stress:

- **Balanced Diet**: Nutrient-rich foods can stabilize energy levels and mood better than sugary, highly processed meals.
- **Regular Movement**: Even if it is just a few minutes a day, consistent activity helps your body handle stress.
- **Adequate Rest**: We covered the importance of sleep in Chapter 8, but it matters here too. Rest is your body's way to recover from daily challenges.
- **Controlled Screen Time**: Spending hours scrolling online can raise stress if you are constantly reading alarming news or comparing yourself to others. Set limits to protect your mental space.

A Simple Daily Routine to Reduce Worry

1. **Morning Check-In (5 Minutes)**
   As soon as you wake up, do a quick mental scan. Note how you feel physically and mentally. If you sense worry, remind yourself: "I have some useful methods to handle today's concerns."
2. **Midday Pause (5–10 Minutes)**
   After lunch or halfway through your day, pause to take a few deep breaths. If stress has built up, write down the biggest worry on a small piece of paper. List one action you can take or one fact that challenges your negative thought. Keep the paper as a reminder.
3. **Early Evening Relaxation (15–20 Minutes)**
   Before jumping into chores or tasks at home, take a short walk, do

light stretching, or have a calm moment of quiet. This transition time can help you release built-up tension from the day.
4. **Bedtime Wind-Down (15–30 Minutes)**
Avoid bright screens, heavy debates, or stressful tasks right before bed. Pick a calming activity—like reading a light book or listening to soft music. If a worry appears, jot it down in a notebook and tell yourself, "I will look at this tomorrow when I am refreshed."

Keeping an Eye on Your Thoughts

Your thoughts greatly affect stress and worry. Sometimes we have "distorted" thoughts—like jumping to the worst possible outcome or labeling ourselves harshly ("I'm so useless because I forgot a small detail!"). Challenge these thoughts by asking:

- **Is there proof for what I'm thinking?**
- **What would I tell a friend if they said this about themselves?**
- **Could there be a more kind or balanced way to see this?**

Often, you will find the worried thought is bigger than the reality.

Staying Motivated to Manage Stress

It can be tempting to ignore stress until it becomes too large to handle. But using even a few methods from this chapter on a regular basis can make life smoother. Remember why you want to lower stress: better health, clearer mind, nicer interactions with loved ones, and more. Write down these reasons and keep them visible. That way, when you feel lazy about practicing relaxation or journaling, you can remind yourself of the benefits.

Chapter Summary

- Stress can come from having too many tasks, facing big changes, or worrying about the future.
- Worry often cycles around "what if" thoughts that may not be based on facts.
- Constant stress and worry can harm the body and mind, leading to tiredness, sadness, and trouble focusing.
- Recognize early signs like a racing heart, tense muscles, and irritability.
- Ease stress by breaking tasks into steps, using time blocks, practicing relaxation, and enjoying activities.
- Limit worry by questioning negative thoughts, scheduling "worry time," and taking action where possible.
- You can handle stress in real time by breathing deeply, using calming self-talk, and staying present in the moment.
- Long-term strategies include using a stress journal, seeking support, organizing your priorities, and practicing gratitude.
- Problem solving differs from worry—one focuses on realistic steps while the other loops on fears.
- Lifestyle choices such as regular movement, balanced diet, and adequate rest reduce chronic stress.
- A daily routine with short check-ins and evening wind-downs can create steady calmness.
- Challenge distorted thoughts by looking for proof or imagining what you would say to a friend in the same situation.
- Keep your motivation strong by remembering how less stress can improve health, mood, and relationships.

By handling stress and worry in a thoughtful way, you open up mental space to enjoy life more fully. These methods will support your self-worth and personal growth, too. In the next chapter, we will explore personal values—how they shape your actions, guide your choices, and play a part in how you see yourself. Understanding your values can help you prioritize what truly matters, which can further reduce stress and build confidence.

CHAPTER 10: PERSONAL VALUES

Personal values are the core beliefs that guide how you act and see the world. They are like an inner compass that helps you decide what is important. When you know your values, you can make choices that fit who you truly are. This sense of alignment can increase self-respect and reduce internal conflict. In this chapter, we will explore what personal values are, how they form, and ways to identify and live by them. We will also discuss the link between values, decision-making, and self-esteem.

What Are Personal Values?

Personal values are beliefs or principles that matter to you at a deep level. They might include honesty, kindness, learning, independence, creativity, or loyalty. Each person's set of values can look different because we learn them from life experiences, family traditions, cultural influences, and personal reflection. Values are not just about what we say is good; they are about what we consistently show is important to us through our choices.

Why Values Matter

1. **Guidance in Decision-Making**
   When you know your key values, you have a framework to decide what to do in tough situations. For example, if honesty is a top value, you will likely choose to tell the truth even when it is hard.
2. **Sense of Purpose**
   Values can give your life direction. If you value helping others, you might volunteer or choose a job where you can support people in need. This purpose can fuel motivation, even when things get tough.
3. **Stronger Self-Worth**
   Acting on your values means you are being true to yourself. This can lead to a sense of wholeness and less self-doubt, because you know you are living in line with what matters most.

4. **Better Boundaries**
   If you recognize that respect is a key value, you will be more likely to set firm limits when someone disrespects you. Knowing your values gives you a clear reason to uphold boundaries.

Where Do Values Come From?

- **Family and Upbringing**: As children, we often absorb values from our parents or caregivers. For instance, if they value hard work, we might develop a strong work ethic.
- **Culture and Society**: Different communities may emphasize certain values, like collective well-being or personal freedom.
- **Personal Experiences**: Major events—like overcoming an illness or traveling—can shape what you find important.
- **Reflection and Learning**: As you grow, you might question the values you grew up with and form new ones based on your own conclusions.

It is normal for values to shift over time as you learn and see more of the world.

Common Examples of Personal Values

- **Honesty**: Telling the truth and being genuine.
- **Kindness**: Acting with care toward others.
- **Fairness**: Wanting equal treatment for all.
- **Curiosity**: Eager to learn and explore.
- **Independence**: Preferring to rely on yourself and make your own choices.
- **Teamwork**: Enjoying shared efforts and group support.
- **Creativity**: Valuing new ideas and original thinking.
- **Faith or Spirituality**: Placing a high importance on spiritual beliefs.
- **Courage**: Standing up for what is right, even when afraid.
- **Respect**: Recognizing everyone's rights and dignity.

This list is not exhaustive, but it shows how values can be quite varied. One person might rank independence first, while another sees teamwork as central to their life.

Identifying Your Own Values

1. **Look at Times You Felt Fulfilled**
   Think of moments you felt truly happy or proud. Ask yourself: "What made that moment special?" Often, the reason is linked to one of your values. For instance, if you felt great after helping a friend move, maybe kindness or service is a key value.
2. **Notice Times You Were Upset**
   Think about situations that made you angry or uneasy. Often, we feel upset when someone violates a value we hold dear. If you felt upset because someone was dishonest, that might indicate honesty is very important to you.
3. **Examine Role Models**
   Who do you admire? What traits do they show? If you look up to someone who always speaks their mind respectfully, it could mean authenticity or respect is a strong value for you.
4. **Use a Values List**
   You can find lists of common personal values online or in self-help books. Read through them and highlight words that resonate with you. This is just a tool—your exact values might not appear on any list, but it can help you get started.
5. **Journaling**
   Write down your thoughts about what matters most to you in life. Do not worry about full sentences or structure. Let the ideas flow. Later, revisit your notes and see if certain themes come up again and again.

Prioritizing Values

You might find you have many values—kindness, honesty, fairness, health, curiosity, family, and so on. Trying to keep them all at the exact same level can be tricky. Sometimes you need to know which ones come first when conflicts arise. For instance, if you value both loyalty and honesty, what happens if a friend does something wrong and asks you to cover for them? Which value would guide your choice?

Try putting your top values in order. This is not set in stone, but it can help you handle real-life dilemmas. You might say, "Honesty comes before loyalty for me," or, "Loyalty to family stands above other values." There is no universal right or wrong here—it is about personal reflection. But clarity on priority can prevent confusion later.

Living by Your Values

1. **Set Goals Aligned with Values**
   If health is a top value, you might aim to exercise regularly or choose meals that support your body. If creativity ranks high, you might set a goal to paint or write a short story each week. Aligning goals with values keeps you motivated even when you face challenges.
2. **Review Choices**
   When you have a major choice—such as accepting a job offer or moving to a new place—ask how it fits your values. If the job pays well but demands you act in ways that clash with honesty, you might feel unhappy later.
3. **Check In Often**
   Life can get busy. It helps to pause every now and then (maybe monthly or quarterly) to ask, "Am I living in line with what matters to me?" If the answer is no, think of small steps to realign your actions with your values.
4. **Be Ready for Sacrifice**
   Sometimes living by a certain value means giving up something else in the short term. For example, valuing honesty might mean telling the truth when it leads to an uncomfortable situation. Over time, these sacrifices can lead to deeper self-respect.

How Values Affect Self-Worth

When your actions clash with your values, you can feel uneasy or guilty. For example, if you cheat on a test but value honesty, you might carry shame that lowers self-esteem. On the other hand, making choices that reflect your values helps you stand firm in who you are. You do not have to pretend or hide. This alignment can increase feelings of self-acceptance.

There is also a sense of stability that comes from living by your values. When the outside world changes or when you face setbacks, your values can remain a solid ground. You might lose a job, but if you know you acted with integrity, you can still feel personal pride.

Dealing with Value Conflicts

Sometimes values can clash. Here are steps to handle it:

1. **Identify the Conflict**
   Name the two values that are fighting for attention. For example, "I want to be loyal to my friend" vs. "I want to be truthful."
2. **Think About Consequences**
   What happens if you honor one value over the other? List possible outcomes. You can do this in a journal or by talking to someone you trust.
3. **Check Your Highest Priority**
   Refer back to your list of top values. Which one do you usually place above the other?
4. **Make a Balanced Choice if Possible**
   Sometimes there is a middle path. For instance, you could be honest with your friend about why you cannot cover for them while still offering them support in another way.
5. **Accept Imperfection**
   There may be no perfect answer. Do your best and remember that you are learning. Even if you make a choice that feels off later, you can learn from it to refine your priorities.

The Influence of Peer and Social Pressures

Society often tries to shape our values. Ads tell us that wealth or looks should be our biggest goals. Friends might tease us if we do not share their interests. Online platforms might glorify fame and clicks. Recognizing these pressures helps you step back and ask, "Is that truly what I value, or am I just going with the flow?" Standing by your own values can be tough, but it leads to more authentic living.

If you find that your social circle consistently pushes you to act against your values, you might need to consider new connections or at least set firm boundaries. Over time, you will likely feel more comfortable around people who accept your values and do not pressure you to abandon them.

Surprising Insights About Values

1. **Values Can Be Negative**
   Sometimes we hold onto harmful principles—like "I must be perfect at all costs." This is a value that can lead to stress and self-criticism. Recognizing a harmful value lets you question and replace it with something healthier.
2. **We Have "Hidden" Values**
   You might think you do not care about status, yet find yourself chasing it to impress others. This means a hidden value might be guiding your behavior. Bringing it to light can help you decide if you really want to keep it.
3. **Values Are Not Always Easy to Put Into Words**
   Some people live by a strong feeling or principle but cannot label it right away. That is okay. Sometimes you have to experiment with describing it before you find the right word.
4. **Micro-Values**
   Some experts talk about "micro-values," which are smaller guiding principles you use in daily life. For example, "greeting coworkers politely each morning" could reflect a small but meaningful principle of friendliness. Paying attention to micro-values can help you see the many ways you live (or do not live) by your beliefs each day.

Practical Exercises for Value Clarity

1. **Write a "Who Am I?" Letter**
   Pretend a friend across the country asks, "What kind of person are you?" Write a short letter describing your core beliefs and what you stand for. Don't worry about perfection—focus on honesty.
2. **Make a "Values Vision Board"**
   Cut out or print images, words, or quotes that resonate with your values. Arrange them on a board or page. This visual display can remind you daily of what is important.
3. **Daily Mini-Reflection**
   Each evening, take one minute to ask yourself: "Did I live in line with my top values today?" If yes, note one example. If no, think about what blocked you and how you might try again tomorrow.
4. **Value-Focused Decisions**
   Next time you have a decision—like accepting a social invite or buying something—ask which value this choice connects to. If you cannot find a link to a value, consider if it is worth doing.

Linking Values to Goals

Values are the why, while goals can be the what and how. For instance, if you value learning (the why), your goal might be to read one book a month or take an online course (the what), and you might schedule reading time or set up a study plan (the how). Without clear values, goals can feel empty. When you tie goals to values, you create a strong inner drive to succeed.

Overcoming Obstacles to Living Your Values

1. **Fear of Judgment**
   You might hesitate to show your true values because friends or family might mock you. Remind yourself that you cannot please

everyone. Over time, living by your values can draw in people who respect the real you.

2. **Procrastination**
   Even if you know what you value, you might put off actions. Break your tasks into smaller steps. Reward yourself for small wins. Keep your values visible so you remember why you want to act.
3. **Doubt About Your Worth**
   Sometimes people think they do not deserve to live by their values. That is not true. Your values matter, and living by them can help build the sense that you are worthy.
4. **Lack of Time or Resources**
   If you value traveling but do not have money right now, you can still honor the spirit of that value by exploring new places locally or reading about different cultures. The idea is to find a way, even if small, to respect what you believe in.

Values in Different Life Areas

- **Relationships**: If you value honesty, you will be honest with friends, family, and partners. If you value kindness, you will look for ways to help or encourage loved ones.
- **Career**: If fairness is a major value, you will want a workplace where people are treated equally. If you value creativity, you will look for roles that allow you to produce new ideas.
- **Health**: If self-care is important, you will find ways to exercise, eat well, and rest, even when busy.
- **Community**: If community service is high on your list, you might volunteer or help your neighborhood in some way.

By mapping your values onto these areas, you see how they connect to everyday life.

Adjusting Values Over Time

Your values might shift as you grow older. For example, you might value adventure in your twenties, focusing on travel or new experiences. Later, you might find that stability or family well-being becomes more important. This is normal. The key is to check in with yourself and recognize these changes. Clinging to values that no longer reflect who you are can cause confusion. Accept that change can happen and adapt as needed.

Handling Criticism of Your Values

Some people might challenge or criticize what you hold dear. They might say you are too idealistic or that you should want different things. Here is how to handle it:

- **Stay Calm**: Breathe and resist the urge to argue harshly.
- **Explain Briefly**: If it feels right, clarify why that value matters to you. You do not have to convince them, just express your perspective.
- **Maintain Respect**: If the other person refuses to respect your values, consider how close you want to be to them. You can still treat them politely while standing your ground.

Sometimes criticism can help you refine your ideas, but it does not have to undermine them unless you choose to change.

Chapter Summary

- Personal values are the core beliefs that guide your behavior and decisions.
- They can come from family, culture, personal experiences, or thoughtful reflection.
- Common examples include honesty, kindness, fairness, curiosity, and independence.

- Identifying your values can be done by looking at moments of fulfillment or upset, studying role models, or using lists.
- Prioritizing values helps you handle conflicts when they arise.
- Living by your values leads to stronger self-worth, as your actions align with your inner beliefs.
- Value clashes can happen; handle them by naming each value, considering outcomes, and checking your highest priorities.
- Peer pressure or social norms might challenge your values, but staying true to them supports your authenticity.
- Some values might be hidden or even harmful; bring them to light and decide if you want to keep them.
- Practical ways to define and maintain values include writing letters, making a vision board, and daily check-ins.
- Values connect to all parts of life: relationships, career, health, and community involvement.
- They can change over time, so it is wise to review and adjust as needed.
- Dealing with criticism of your values involves calm responses and self-assurance.

Understanding your personal values is a big step toward living a life that feels right for you. When you align your day-to-day choices with your values, you reduce internal conflicts and gain a sense of direction. In the chapters ahead, we will look at setting realistic goals and breaking patterns that keep you stuck. These ideas will tie in closely with the concept of values, because your goals become more meaningful when they spring from what you find most important.

CHAPTER 11: SETTING REALISTIC GOALS

Goals help you decide where you want to go in life. They give you direction so you do not wander around feeling unsure. But if your goals are too big, you can end up feeling overwhelmed. If they are too easy, you might not grow much. In this chapter, we will look at why it is important to pick goals that stretch you a bit but still feel possible. We will also discuss how to handle setbacks without giving up. By the end, you should feel more confident about choosing targets you can reach step by step.

---

1. Why Having Goals Matters

It is normal to wonder why we need goals in the first place. Some people feel it is easier to just let life happen. But having goals can:

1. **Bring Clarity**: Goals give shape to your day. Instead of waking up and feeling aimless, you know you have tasks that lead toward something you care about.
2. **Grow Your Abilities**: Goals push you to learn new skills. Whether it is studying a language or improving at a sport, you use effort in a focused way.
3. **Boost Self-Esteem**: Each small win builds your sense of worth. Seeing progress reminds you that you can make changes in your life.
4. **Give a Sense of Control**: Sometimes life feels random. Goals let you decide what you want to do. This can reduce feeling helpless when things around you shift.

---

2. What Makes a Goal "Realistic"?

A realistic goal is challenging enough to help you grow but not so huge that it feels impossible. For example, saying, "I want to become a rock star by next week" is not realistic for most people. But saying, "I want to learn three new songs on the guitar this month" might be realistic. It includes a clear aim (three songs) and a timeline (a month). You can see it is something you can do with regular practice.

But keep in mind, "realistic" does not mean "easy." It means the goal has a good chance of success if you stick with it. A bit of a challenge is helpful because it keeps you interested. If a goal is too easy, you will not feel much excitement about finishing it. If it is too big, you might feel anxious and give up early.

3. Looking at "Too Big" vs. "Too Small" Goals

1. **Too Big**: Imagine you set out to run a marathon next month but you have never jogged before. This can lead to injury or quitting because it feels too far from your current level. You might also feel disappointed if you cannot meet the target.
2. **Too Small**: If your goal is something you can do with no effort—like doing two push-ups in a whole week—maybe that is too easy. You will not see real progress, so you will not build new skills or confidence.
3. **Finding the Middle**: The sweet spot is a goal that makes you think, "This is a bit tough, but I can see a path to do it." Maybe you commit to jogging three times a week for 20 minutes if you are new to running. That might be enough to push you while still being doable.

4. The Power of Breaking Goals into Steps

Large goals can feel scary when you look at them as one giant task. Breaking them into parts can help:

- **Less Overwhelm**: Instead of seeing a huge mountain, you see small hills. Each hill is a piece of the bigger goal.
- **Clear Focus**: With steps written down, you know exactly what to do next. This prevents the frozen feeling of not knowing where to begin.
- **Celebrating Wins**: Each time you complete one step, you get a small feeling of success. This keeps you motivated.

For instance, if your goal is to write a short story, you can break it into steps:

1. Plan your main characters.

2. Write a rough outline of the plot.
3. Draft the first section.
4. Draft the middle section.
5. Draft the final section.
6. Edit your draft.
7. Show it to a friend or teacher for feedback.

Each of these steps feels smaller than "Write a story from scratch." When you finish one step, you can check it off your list and feel that sense of progress.

---

5. Staying Motivated Day by Day

Even with a realistic goal, it can be hard to stay motivated. That is normal. Excitement often comes in waves. Here are some tips:

1. **Remember Your "Why"**: If you know the reason you set the goal, you can return to that whenever motivation drops. For example, if your goal is to learn a new language, maybe your "why" is to speak with a friend who lives in another country.
2. **Track Progress**: Use a notebook or an app to mark each day's work. Seeing a list of days you practiced can push you to keep going so you do not break the chain.
3. **Reward Yourself**: Give yourself something small to look forward to after you hit a milestone. It could be a special snack or a break to do something fun.
4. **Find Accountability**: If you tell a friend or group about your goal, you might be more likely to stick with it. You can update them on how things are going. Sometimes sharing your plan adds a bit of healthy pressure to keep going.

---

6. Handling Setbacks Without Quitting

No matter how realistic your goal is, there will be bumps along the road. Maybe you get sick for a week or you have sudden responsibilities at home. Here is how to handle such moments:

1. **Review Your Goal**: Check if your original timeline needs adjusting. If you aimed to finish in two weeks but got sick, maybe extend it to three weeks. Adjusting is not failure—it is being practical.
2. **Avoid the "All or Nothing" Thought**: It is easy to think, "I missed three days, so I might as well quit." But missing a few days is not the end. Think of progress like climbing steps. Even if you slip, you do not start back at the ground floor.
3. **Forgive Mistakes**: Beating yourself up often leads to dropping the goal entirely. Instead, accept that mistakes happen and keep going.
4. **Seek Help**: If you hit a block, talk to someone who has done something similar. They might have fresh tips or encourage you to approach the task differently.

---

7. Setting Different Kinds of Goals

Not all goals are the same. Some are about daily habits, others are about major achievements. Understanding different types can help you pick what fits your life:

- **Short-Term Goals**: Things you want to do soon—like finishing a school project or learning a short dance routine. They might take a few days or weeks.
- **Long-Term Goals**: These are bigger. You might want to save money for a future trip or train for a sports competition next year. They require a longer plan and consistent effort.
- **Skill-Based Goals**: For example, learning a programming language, improving drawing skills, or becoming a better speaker.
- **Lifestyle Goals**: Aiming to change your daily routine, such as waking up earlier, cooking healthier meals, or spending less time on social media.

Each type of goal might need a slightly different approach. Long-term goals often need smaller milestones along the way, while short-term goals can be done quicker but might need intense focus for a brief period.

---

8. Avoiding Comparison with Others

One trap is looking at a friend or stranger online who seems far ahead. You might feel your goals are silly compared to theirs. But each person has their own situation. Comparing can hurt your confidence and make you lose sight of why you set your goals in the first place. Instead, focus on your own gains. If last month you could only do five push-ups and now you can do ten, that is real progress—no matter if someone else can do 50.

9. Handling Negative Opinions

Sometimes people around you might question your goals. They might say, "That's pointless," or "You can't do that." Hearing negativity can shake you, but remember that a realistic goal does not require everyone else's approval. While feedback can sometimes be helpful—if it is constructive—constant negativity is not. You can:

1. **Set Boundaries**: If someone is always putting you down, avoid talking about your goals with them.
2. **Seek Support**: Find people who encourage you. This might be a teacher, a counselor, or online communities that share your interests.
3. **Remember Your Own Judgment**: You have weighed your strengths and chosen a goal that fits you. You do not need to please everyone.

10. Using "Mini-Goals" for Motivation

One special tip is to set mini-goals within a larger goal. For instance, if you want to read 12 books in a year, you can have a mini-goal of reading one book each month. Each time you hit that monthly target, you can do a small celebration inside your mind ("I did it!") or treat yourself in a simple way. Breaking the main target into these monthly parts can keep you energized.

These mini-goals work well because they cut down the wait time for feeling accomplished. Instead of waiting an entire year to see if you met your target, you get a success moment every few weeks.

11. The Role of Habits in Reaching Goals

Many goals depend on daily habits. If your goal is to get better at math, you might need a habit of doing 20 minutes of practice every day. Without a habit, you rely on motivation alone, which can go up and down. Habits, by contrast, become part of your normal routine. Over time, it becomes easier to stick to your plan because it is almost automatic.

- **Start Small**: If you are not used to studying daily, begin with 10 minutes. Later, you can increase it to 20 or 30.
- **Link a New Habit to an Old One**: If you always have breakfast in the morning, you can plan to study right after you finish eating. This link helps the new habit stick.
- **Keep Track**: Mark each day you follow the habit in a calendar or an app. This visual proof can be motivating.

12. When to Adjust or Drop a Goal

Sometimes you might realize a goal no longer fits your life. Maybe you set it based on old interests, or new priorities appear. Letting go of a goal can feel like defeat, but it is not always. If the goal truly does not match your life anymore, adjusting or dropping it can free you to pursue something that matters more to you now. Ask these questions:

1. **Do I still care about this goal?**
2. **Does it align with what I want from life at this point?**
3. **Have I learned what I needed to from this goal?**

If the answer suggests it is time to move on, do it without self-blame. It is a natural part of growth to refine what we aim for as we learn more about ourselves.

13. Keeping Goals Flexible

Life is unpredictable. That is why flexibility is a key piece of any realistic goal. Maybe you planned to do a certain project over the weekend, but a family emergency came up. You can shift your timeline rather than feeling like you failed. Being flexible does not mean you abandon the goal; it means you adapt to life's changes. This approach helps you handle surprises without giving up completely.

---

14. Unique Tips for Setting Goals

Below are some less-discussed tips:

1. **Visual Reminders**: Create a small sign or picture that represents your goal and place it where you will see it every day—maybe on your desk or fridge.
2. **Future You Thinking**: Ask yourself how you want to feel in three months or a year. Will finishing this goal help you reach that feeling? This future-thinking can spark motivation.
3. **Multiple Pathways**: For bigger goals, list more than one way to reach them. If one path hits a dead end, you can switch to another without losing time.
4. **Involve Your Senses**: If you want to remember your goal better, link it to a sense. For example, wear a certain wristband whenever you work on that goal. That physical reminder can keep you focused.
5. **Test the Waters**: Before committing fully to a big goal, try a short "preview." For example, if you think you want to learn guitar, borrow one for a week to see if you like practicing.

---

15. Real-Life Example of Setting a Realistic Goal

Imagine a high school student who wants to improve in science. They decide they want to raise their grade in biology from a low mark to a decent mark by the end of the semester. They sit down and plan:

1. **Small Steps**: They will watch one short video on the topic each evening and take quick notes.
2. **Weekly Checks**: At the end of each week, they do a practice quiz.
3. **Ask for Help**: They talk to the teacher after class once a week with any questions.
4. **Adjust**: If they see good progress after a month, they continue. If not, they might add a study group or spend an extra 30 minutes on weekends.

This is a realistic plan because it has clear steps, built-in checks, and room to change if needed. The student is not forcing themselves to go from a failing grade to the top of the class in one week. Instead, they use consistent effort over time.

---

16. The Difference Between Dreams and Goals

A dream is a vision of what you want someday. It might be large or wonderful, but it is not yet a plan. A goal is more concrete. It includes a real start time, a method, and often a finish date or at least a checkpoint. Dreams can be exciting, but turning a dream into a goal means figuring out the details. That is the difference between saying, "I want to be a great cook," and saying, "I will practice one new recipe each week and note what works best."

---

17. Tools You Can Use

1. **Calendar**: Mark deadlines or practice days to keep yourself on schedule.
2. **Whiteboard or Sticky Notes**: Keep your steps visible. Move them from "To Do" to "Done" as you finish each.
3. **Timer Apps**: Use short focused sessions (like 20–30 minutes). Stop and rest. Repeat. This helps if you struggle with distractions.
4. **Bullet Journal**: Some people use bullet journals to record daily tasks and keep track of long-term targets.

5. **Online Support**: Many sites or communities let you share your progress. Posting updates might help you stick to the plan.

18. Learning from Each Goal Attempt

Even if a goal ends up half-finished, there is still a lesson in it. Maybe you realize you need a more detailed step-by-step plan next time, or you need a buddy to keep you on track. Each attempt builds knowledge for future goals. This is why you should not see an unfinished goal as a full failure—it can be a step that prepares you for success with a new plan.

19. The Value of Reflection

Reflection means taking a moment, maybe each week or month, to see how your plans are going. Ask yourself:

- **What did I accomplish this period?**
- **What went well? What got in the way?**
- **How do I feel about my progress?**
- **Do I need to change my steps or my timeline?**

Reflection can stop small issues from growing bigger because you spot them early. It also makes you aware of positive changes you might have overlooked.

20. Putting It All Together

Setting realistic goals starts with deciding what you want and why. Next, you break the goal into parts, make a timeline, and think about how to track progress. You also remain open to adjusting if life throws unexpected events at you. Along the way, you celebrate small wins in your mind and learn from any slip-ups.

This chapter showed you how to keep your goals within reach without making them so easy that they do not help you grow. The main point is to balance challenge with common sense. Remember that a single missed day is not the end. A realistic goal is one you can keep working on steadily. With patience and clever planning, you will see real results.

Chapter 11 Summary

- **Realistic goals help you learn and avoid the trap of feeling it is impossible.**
- **Breaking big goals into smaller steps prevents overwhelm and boosts motivation.**
- **Motivation can rise and fall; use methods like progress tracking and small rewards to stay on course.**
- **Setbacks are normal; adjust your plan or timeline rather than quitting.**
- **Different goals (short-term, long-term, skill-based, lifestyle) need different plans.**
- **Steer clear of constant comparison and harsh negativity from others.**
- **Use mini-goals and smart habits to keep moving, and know when it is time to change a goal.**
- **Tools like calendars, timers, and bullet journals can help you stay organized.**
- **Reflections keep you aware of what is working and what to fix.**
- **A realistic goal is not always easy, but it should be possible with steady effort.**

Next, we will look at how to break old habits and patterns that block you from reaching these goals. Even with the best plan, repeating old actions can hold you back. By learning new tricks to replace unhelpful routines, you will find it easier to move toward the future you want.

CHAPTER 12: BREAKING OLD PATTERNS

Many people try to improve their lives but find themselves trapped by old behaviors. They might start a new routine, only to slip back into the same habits. Why is it so hard to let go of old patterns? And what can you do to truly change? This chapter explores the reasons we hold on to familiar habits, how to recognize them, and ways to create better routines that last. With consistent action, you can break free from behaviors that keep you stuck.

1. What Are Old Patterns?

Old patterns are behaviors or mindsets you repeat without even thinking. They might include:

- **Avoiding tasks until the last minute.**
- **Eating for comfort when upset.**
- **Procrastinating on projects despite wanting to do them.**
- **Staying quiet even when you have something important to share.**
- **Speaking harshly to yourself whenever you make a small mistake.**

These actions often become so normal that you barely notice them. But they can block your progress and lower your self-esteem.

2. Why We Cling to Old Ways

If an action causes problems, why do we keep doing it? There are some common reasons:

1. **Familiarity**: The habit is something we know. Even if it is harmful, it feels "safe" because it is part of our routine.
2. **Short-Term Comfort**: Some patterns give a quick relief (like procrastinating feels easier in the moment, even though it leads to stress later).

3. **Fear of Change**: Trying new approaches can be scary. People might worry, "What if I fail with the new method?" so they stick to old ways.
4. **Lack of Awareness**: Some folks do not realize how much their habits affect their lives until someone points it out.

Recognizing these reasons is the first step to breaking them. Once you see why you cling to old patterns, you can find better ways to handle those fears or needs.

---

3. Spotting Your Own Patterns

How do you know which habits to break? First, become aware of how you spend your time and react to stress. You can try:

- **Journaling**: Write down your day in a simple log. Note when you procrastinated, when you felt bored or upset, and what you did.
- **Checking Emotional Triggers**: Notice which feelings lead to certain actions. For example, do you often scroll on social media when you feel anxious?
- **Asking Friends or Family**: Sometimes people close to you see patterns you miss. A friend might say, "You always cancel plans whenever you have had a tough day."

Write these observations somewhere safe. The goal is not to feel bad about yourself, but to identify what you often repeat.

---

4. Replacing vs. Removing

One important trick is that it is often easier to replace a habit than to just remove it. If you simply try to stop doing something without putting a new behavior in its place, you create a void. That void can feel unsettling, making it more likely you will go back to the old habit. For example:

- **Old Habit**: Eating junk food when bored.

- **New Choice**: Reaching for fruit or a glass of water, or doing a quick stretch when bored.

By swapping in a better habit, you give your mind and body an alternative that meets a similar need (managing boredom), but in a healthier way.

---

5. Breaking Patterns Step by Step

1. **Pinpoint One Habit to Change**: Do not try to fix everything at once. Pick a single pattern—maybe you want to stop staying up too late.
2. **Understand the Trigger**: If you watch videos until midnight, is it because you are stressed or because you lose track of time?
3. **Plan a Replacement**: Decide on something else to do instead of the old habit. Perhaps you will set an alarm at 10 PM to remind you to turn off devices and read a light book.
4. **Practice**: Begin with a short trial period—like one week—and track your progress daily.
5. **Adjust**: If you fail half the time, ask why. Maybe you need a better method, like putting your phone in another room. Keep tweaking until you find a routine that works more often than not.

---

6. Handling Cravings for the Old Way

When you try to break an old behavior, you might feel a pull to go back. This is normal. The mind likes what is known. Here are some tips to manage these urges:

1. **Wait It Out**: Often, the urge will peak and then pass if you do not act on it right away. Tell yourself you will wait five minutes before giving in. During that time, do a short task, like washing dishes or organizing a small drawer.
2. **Remind Yourself of Consequences**: Think about why you wanted to change in the first place. If you go back to the old habit, what problems might return?

3. **Use Encouraging Thoughts**: Speak to yourself as you would to a friend. "I know this is hard, but I can get through it."
4. **Limit Access**: Make it harder to do the old habit. If you tend to snack at night, do not keep junk food in your room. If you overspend online, remove saved credit card details so you must type them in each time.

---

7. The "If-Then" Planning Method

A strong technique for habit change is "If-Then" planning. You decide in advance how you will handle triggers. For example:

- **If** I feel stressed about homework, **then** I will do five minutes of deep breathing before starting.
- **If** I start scrolling on social media after 10 PM, **then** I will shut it down and read a few pages of a book.

This approach helps because it gives your brain a clear instruction for what to do when the problem moment arrives. Instead of having to decide on the spot, you already have a plan.

---

8. Hidden Ways We Sabotage Ourselves

Sometimes we break progress by:

- **Making Excuses**: We say, "Just this once won't hurt." Over time, these "once" moments pile up.
- **Seeking Comfort**: When stressed or upset, we fall back on the old pattern because it feels safer.
- **Not Preparing**: We do not remove items or situations that trigger the habit. For instance, if you want to stop late-night gaming, but your system is in your bedroom, it is easier to slip back.

The solution is to be honest with ourselves. If an environment or mindset keeps pushing us toward the old pattern, we must rearrange the setting or plan how to handle those moments. Sometimes this means changing our surroundings or reducing time with people who tempt us to repeat the old habit.

9. Celebrating Small Shifts in Behavior

When trying to break a long-standing pattern, even a small shift is worth noticing. Maybe you used to skip brushing your teeth before bed half the time. Now you skip it only once a week. That is improvement, even if it is not perfect yet. Recognize these small gains. They help your mind see that change is happening, which boosts confidence to continue.

10. Changing Patterns in Relationships

Sometimes old behaviors involve how we treat or respond to others. For example, maybe you always shut down during an argument, or you let others speak over you. Changing these patterns requires open communication:

1. **Be Clear About the Pattern**: If you tend to avoid talking about problems, let the person know you are trying to do better.
2. **Agree on Signals**: If you want to speak up more in conversations, tell a friend to gently tap your arm if they notice you staying silent out of habit. This external cue can help you shift your response.
3. **Offer Reminders**: If the pattern is something you do together—like a parent-child homework conflict—decide on a code word to pause the old behavior. For instance, if either of you says "Pause," it means everyone should take a breath before continuing.

11. Time Needed for Real Change

There is no exact number of days for a habit to become your new normal. Some people say it takes about three weeks, others say longer. The truth is it depends on the person and the habit. But keep in mind:

- **It Might Be Rocky at First**: The first days can feel awkward or forced. That is normal.
- **Some Days Are Easier**: After a while, the new habit might start to feel less forced.
- **Mistakes Happen**: Even months into a new routine, you might slip once in a while. That is not a reason to quit.

Think of it like training a muscle in the body. You will not become super strong overnight. You need regular practice.

---

12. Golden Gems to Stay on Track

Below are some special tips you might not hear about every day:

1. **Habit Stacking**: Attach the new habit to something you already do. For example, if you want to practice gratitude, do it right after you brush your teeth each morning.
2. **Tiny Tests**: If you want to break a pattern of playing video games for hours, start by cutting just 10 minutes of game time each day. Over a month, that could be 300 minutes saved without a drastic overnight change.
3. **Accountability Buddy**: Find someone who also wants to break a habit or form a new one. Check in regularly. Hearing about their struggles and wins can keep you motivated.
4. **Visual Progress Board**: Post a chart on your wall. Each day you stick to your new routine, color in a box. Seeing a chain of colored boxes can be surprisingly powerful.
5. **Talk to Your Future Self**: Write a short note from your future self who has already broken the old pattern. What would they say to you about how life improved? This mind trick can remind you that your efforts matter.

---

13. Dealing with Guilt from Old Patterns

You might feel guilty about how long you have had a certain habit. Maybe you blame yourself for not changing sooner. This guilt can pull you down and make you think, "What is the point? I have messed up for years." Instead, view the past as a teacher. You learned how certain habits do not work for you. Now you are taking steps toward improvement. That is more productive than staying stuck in regret.

---

14. Balancing Rules with Kindness

Some people try to break patterns by setting very strict rules. For example, "I will never eat any sugar again!" While strong limits can help, be careful not to create a situation that is too harsh. If you make the rules too strict, you might rebel against them. A moderate approach often works better: "I will cut back on sugary snacks to once a week," rather than "None, ever." Overly strict rules can lead to frustration if you slip, which might push you back into old habits.

---

15. The Role of Identity

Changing how you see yourself can help a lot. If you label yourself as "a lazy person," you might keep acting that way because you believe it is who you are. But if you shift to "I am someone who is learning to be more active," you open the door for new actions. Words you use about yourself can shape your mindset. Choose them wisely.

---

16. Outside Triggers vs. Inner Triggers

Some triggers for old patterns come from your environment—like a coworker who always tempts you with treats if you are trying to eat healthier. Others come from within—like feeling sad or bored. To handle outside triggers, you might change your setting (avoid the snack area or ask coworkers not to offer you sweets). For inner triggers, you can practice emotional skills such as naming your feeling ("I'm bored"), then picking a better action ("I'll do a puzzle for a few minutes").

17. Seeking Professional Support

If an old habit is tied to deeper issues like trauma or strong emotional pain, it may be wise to reach out to a counselor or therapist. They can help you explore why certain patterns formed and guide you in a safe way. There is no shame in asking for expert help. Sometimes a habit is just the surface sign of a bigger matter that needs care.

18. Long-Term Maintenance

Breaking a pattern is one step, but keeping it away is another. You might do well for a month, only to slip back in times of stress. This does not mean you failed. It means you may need a plan for high-stress moments. Ask yourself, "When I am super busy or upset, what can I do instead of returning to my old pattern?" Plan those fallback options in advance. For instance, if you start feeling the urge to do the old behavior, you might call a friend or read a calming story as a quick break.

19. Reassessing Periodically

Over time, you can look at the habit you replaced. Is your new method still working? Do you need to update it? Maybe your schedule changed, or a new stress popped up. Reassessing means you keep fine-tuning your approach. Sometimes people think, "I fixed that problem, so I'm done," but life is always moving. Stay open to making small changes so you can keep the new pattern strong.

20. Connecting This to Self-Worth

Breaking old patterns is a form of self-respect. It says, "I do not have to be stuck forever. I am worth the effort it takes to change." Each time you choose a healthier or more positive action, you reinforce the message that you can grow. Over the weeks and months, these changes can have a large effect on how you see yourself.

Putting It All Together

Breaking old ways is rarely an instant fix. It takes mindful effort, some planning, and a bit of self-kindness to get through bumps along the way. But each time you notice and replace an unhelpful habit with something more positive, you build new connections in your mind. Over time, the healthier behavior can become your new norm.

Change is possible. That does not mean it is always easy, but with patience, support, and the methods listed here, you can free yourself from patterns that hold you back. Then you will be more able to reach the realistic goals you set.

Chapter 12 Summary

- Old patterns are repeated actions or mindsets that can keep you from moving forward.
- We cling to them for comfort, fear of change, or simply because they are familiar.
- Spot your habits by journaling, watching emotional triggers, or asking close ones for feedback.
- Replacing is often easier than just removing. If you stop one behavior, try putting a better one in its place.
- Step-by-step methods—pinpoint the habit, learn the trigger, plan a replacement, practice, adjust—can help you succeed.

- Urges to return to the old pattern will happen, but waiting them out or limiting access can help.
- "If-Then" planning can prepare you for moments of weakness or triggers.
- Watch out for hidden ways you sabotage yourself, like making excuses or not changing your environment.
- Celebrate small improvements because they show you are headed in the right direction.
- Changing patterns in relationships may need clear communication and outside reminders.
- No set rule exists for how many days it takes to form a new habit; it varies by person and situation.
- Use special tips like habit stacking, tiny tests, and visual progress boards to keep going.
- Balance strictness with kindness, because overly harsh rules can cause pushback.
- Shifting your identity language can open you up to acting differently.
- Some triggers come from outside, others from inside feelings, so address both.
- Professional help is valuable if the pattern connects to deeper emotional issues.
- Keep a plan for high-stress times, and reassess your new habits as life changes.
- Breaking old habits supports your self-worth by showing you are capable of growth.

With old patterns beginning to loosen their hold, you can make clearer progress on your goals. In the next chapters, we will look at building good habits and also tackle fears that block us from trying new things. Each chapter connects to the idea of self-improvement and learning to treat ourselves with fairness. By letting go of repeated actions that do not serve you, you free up energy to become the person you truly want to be.

CHAPTER 13: BUILDING GOOD HABITS

Building good habits is a strong way to change your life without depending only on short bursts of willpower. A habit is something you do often until it becomes almost automatic, like brushing your teeth or tying your shoes. When you have many good habits, they make your day flow more smoothly. You save mental energy because you do not have to push yourself to do the right thing each time; it becomes part of your usual routine. This chapter will explain what habits are, why they matter, and how to form ones that support your goals. It will also cover how to handle problems that come up and how to keep going even when life gets busy.

1. Why Good Habits Matter

1. **They Reduce Daily Stress**
   If you have a habit of cleaning up your space each night, you do not wake up to a messy room. It takes less effort to maintain order when you do small actions regularly, rather than one big clean-up once a month. This saves you from the stress of facing a huge chore later.
2. **They Support Larger Goals**
   Good habits are building blocks that help you reach bigger targets in your life. For instance, if you aim to get fit, having a habit of daily exercise means you do not have to push yourself to do a random workout only when you feel guilty. Instead, it is part of your daily schedule.
3. **They Free Up Mental Energy**
   When a behavior is automatic, your brain does not have to debate about it each time. This is why having a set bedtime routine helps you sleep better: you do it without overthinking, and your body recognizes the signals that it is time to rest.
4. **They Improve Self-Worth**
   Each day that you follow a good habit, you show yourself that you can stick to something beneficial. This can build confidence over time. You start to see yourself as someone who can choose well and follow through.

2. Understanding What a Habit Is

A habit starts with a trigger (also called a cue). This trigger could be a certain time, place, or emotional state. For instance, the moment you wake up can be a trigger to brush your teeth. After that, the action (brushing) follows. Once you finish, you often get a reward, like a fresh feeling in your mouth or a sense of being ready for the day.

Over time, your brain links the trigger, the action, and the reward. This chain makes the behavior more automatic. You do not have to think, "Should I brush my teeth?" because the pattern is already in place. This same process can form both helpful and unhelpful habits.

3. How Habits Form and Stick

Habits form faster when there is a clear connection between the trigger, the behavior, and a positive outcome. For example:

- **Trigger**: You walk into your room at night and see your bed.
- **Behavior**: You do your nightly tidy-up, such as folding clothes or picking items off the floor.
- **Reward**: You feel at ease seeing a neat space. You also feel proud for sticking to your plan.

If you skip the tidy-up, you might feel a bit unsettled. Over time, your mind starts to associate bedtime with the quick clean-up. This three-part loop (trigger, behavior, reward) is one key to building good habits.

4. Picking Which Habits to Build

Before you start trying to form new habits, think about what would help you the most. Some habits may look good in theory but may not match your actual needs. A few ideas include:

- **Health Habits**: Such as taking a short walk each day, stretching in the morning, or choosing water instead of sugary drinks.
- **Work or Study Habits**: Setting aside 30 minutes for reading or homework after dinner each night.
- **Personal Growth Habits**: Writing a few lines in a journal, practicing a creative skill, or reviewing your day's successes each evening.
- **Relationship Habits**: Calling a loved one once a week, sending a kind note to a friend, or checking in on a family member regularly.

Ask yourself which area of life you would most like to see improve. Then pick one or two habits in that area. It is easier to begin small than to try changing everything at once.

5. Starting Small: The Key to Success

One reason many people fail at building habits is they aim too high at first. For example, they decide to exercise an hour every day, even though they have never had a workout habit before. That is a big leap. When motivation is high, it may work for a few days, but as soon as life gets in the way or energy is low, the habit falls apart.

Starting small means picking an action that feels so easy you can do it even on a bad day. If you want to write more, maybe set a target of writing for just five minutes each morning. If you want to move more, commit to five squats before you shower. Once the habit is established, you can slowly increase the time or intensity. This approach creates a solid foundation.

6. Linking a New Habit to Something You Already Do

A helpful trick is to tie a new habit to something that is already part of your routine. This is often called "habit stacking." For example:

- **After I brush my teeth at night, I will do 10 minutes of reading before I go to bed.**

- Once I finish washing the dishes in the evening, I will sit down and review my goals for tomorrow.
- Right after I eat breakfast, I will do a quick stretch.

Because the existing action (like brushing your teeth or finishing the dishes) is already in your daily life, attaching a new behavior to it can make the new one more likely to stick.

---

7. Rewarding Yourself in Healthy Ways

Rewards are a big part of the habit loop. They help your brain link the new behavior with something good. But not all rewards have to be big or unhealthy. Some small reward ideas:

- **A Simple Smile**: Take a moment to feel proud after you do the habit. That internal feeling of success is a reward in itself.
- **Visual Tracking**: Put a sticker on a chart each day you do the habit. Seeing those stickers add up can feel good.
- **A Calm Break**: After completing your habit, allow yourself 5 minutes of something peaceful, like listening to a favorite tune.
- **Sharing Progress**: Tell a friend or family member you completed your habit for the day. Their positive feedback can boost your mood.

Over time, the habit might become its own reward. For instance, people who build a running habit often find they feel good after a run. The energy lift itself becomes enough reward to keep going.

---

8. Handling Boredom or Lack of Motivation

Even the best habits can feel boring after a while. Here are ways to manage that:

1. **Mix It Up**: If your habit is exercising, try different routines each week. If your habit is reading, pick various kinds of books or articles. Variety keeps things from feeling stale.

2. **Track Progress**: Seeing small improvements can reignite your interest. If you are learning an instrument, record yourself once a week. Later, you can hear how your playing has improved.
3. **Pair It with Another Activity**: If your habit is something like cleaning, you can listen to a fun podcast while you clean. This adds a bit of enjoyment.
4. **Remember the Purpose**: Think about the bigger reason you started. Maybe you want better health or a more organized space. That purpose can push you when you are tired.

---

9. Dealing with Setbacks

Missing a day or two does not have to ruin your habit. It is important to get back on track as soon as you can. One missed day can be viewed as a reminder that you are human. Two missed days can start to weaken the habit. The key is not to turn it into a week or month of no action.

- **Avoid All-or-Nothing Thinking**: If you miss your usual 30 minutes, do 5 minutes instead. A small effort can keep the pattern alive.
- **Identify the Cause**: If you missed your habit because you were too busy, maybe you need to schedule it earlier or later. If you were too tired, maybe you need to pick a simpler action for that day.
- **Show Self-Kindness**: Talk to yourself gently. "I missed a day, but I can start again now." Harsh self-blame can lead to giving up.

---

10. Combining Habits for Bigger Gains

Once you are comfortable with one habit, you can add another. Over time, these small changes add up. Imagine you form a habit of reading 10 minutes each night, and you also build a habit of taking a daily walk. That is a total of about 70 minutes of reading per week and 7 walks per week, which can lead to more knowledge and better health. This process of stacking good habits can shape your routine in a positive way.

11. Common Mistakes to Avoid

1. **Taking on Too Much at Once**: Trying to form five new habits in a single week usually leads to overload. Focus on one or two key habits at first.
2. **Not Preparing for Obstacles**: Life will throw curveballs—like sudden errands or a change in schedule. If you have a backup plan (for example, a shorter version of your habit), you can keep moving forward.
3. **Comparing with Others**: Your habit-building pace is yours alone. If a friend can run 5 miles every morning but you are starting with 5 minutes of walking, that is okay. Focus on your path.
4. **Lack of Rewards**: If you do not give yourself any sense of satisfaction, your mind may not see why this habit is good. Even a simple, positive thought about yourself can serve as a reward.

12. Habit Contracts and Accountability

Some people like to create a small "habit contract." They write down the habit, why it matters, and what steps they will take. Then they sign it and ask a trusted friend to sign it as a witness. This adds a sense of seriousness to the process.

Accountability can also help. This can look like:

- **Weekly Check-Ins**: Telling a friend or family member each week how many times you did your habit.
- **Online Communities**: Joining a group where people share their habit progress. Hearing others' stories can inspire you to continue.
- **Professional Help**: If the habit is related to a health issue (like a better diet), a coach or nutritionist can support you. If it is about studying, a tutor might be an accountability partner.

13. Tiny Steps vs. Big Jumps

Some goals seem to need big actions. For instance, if you want to lose a large amount of weight or learn a new language. But even these major tasks are more sustainable when broken into smaller daily habits:

- **Learn a Language**: Study for 15 minutes each day, watch a short show in that language, or practice new words for 5 minutes. Over months, these daily actions add up.
- **Weight Management**: Start with small habits like drinking water before meals or taking a short walk daily. As these become natural, you can add more steps.

Big jumps sometimes work, but they also carry a higher risk of burnout. Tiny, steady steps usually lead to more lasting changes.

---

14. Emotions and Habit Building

Our emotions can support or weaken habits. If you feel sad or stressed, you might skip the habit. On the other hand, if you tie the habit to a comforting feeling, it becomes easier to do. For instance, if you decide to do 5 minutes of quiet meditation after work, you might light a softly scented candle or wear cozy clothes. This calming atmosphere can make the habit more appealing, so you are more likely to stick with it.

---

15. Watching Out for Triggers That Harm Good Habits

Sometimes an outside event can trigger a slip back into old patterns. For example, if you are trying to build a habit of writing each morning but then you get a text message from a friend, you might pick up your phone and lose an hour chatting. You can reduce such triggers by:

- **Turning Off Non-Essential Notifications**: This stops random pings from pulling you away.

- **Setting a Clear Time Window**: For instance, "I will write from 7 AM to 7:30 AM, and I will not check my phone until 7:30 AM."
- **Preparing Your Space**: Keep your writing desk tidy, with your notes ready. This helps you dive into the habit quickly instead of searching for pens and paper.

16. Changing Habits in Different Settings

You might find it easier to keep a habit at home but struggle with it when you travel or visit a friend's place. In a new environment, triggers change. Prepare by creating a small kit or plan. For example, if your habit is to do 10 minutes of exercise daily, pack a resistance band or find a short workout you can do anywhere. If your habit is reading, keep a digital book on your phone or a paperback in your bag. That way, you can keep up the habit even in a different place.

17. Setting Time Limits for Better Focus

If you are trying to build a study or reading habit, consider using time blocks. For instance, you might work or study for 20 minutes, then take a 5-minute stretch or water break. This approach, often called a "time-block technique," helps you stay focused and also allows small rests. Knowing a break is coming can make the work block feel more manageable, and it helps your mind stay fresh.

18. Examples of Simple Good Habits

1. **Morning Stretch**: Right after you get out of bed, do a brief stretch routine for a couple of minutes to wake up your muscles.
2. **Drinking Water**: Keep a glass of water by your bed or your desk. Make a habit of sipping water every hour or so.

3. **Note-Taking**: Keep a small notebook handy. Whenever an idea or to-do comes to mind, write it down immediately to avoid forgetting.
4. **Reading Before Sleep**: Replace 10 minutes of phone browsing with 10 minutes of reading a book.
5. **Daily Gratitude Thought**: Each evening, think of one thing that made you feel good that day. This simple act can lift your mood over time.

These may seem small, but done daily, they can support mental health, creativity, and overall well-being.

---

19. Adapting Habits as You Grow

Once a habit becomes easy, you might decide to make it more challenging. For example:

- **If you started walking 10 minutes a day**, you can step it up to 15 minutes or add short jog intervals.
- **If you formed a habit of writing 5 minutes each night**, you might push it to 10 or 15 minutes, or start a small blog.

Adapting habits keeps them from getting stale and matches your growing abilities. However, be sure to change them slowly, so you do not burn out. Jumping from 10 minutes to an hour can be too big a jump, so pick a step that you can realistically handle.

---

20. Bringing Others Along

If you share a space with others, your habits might affect them, or they might affect you. Maybe you want a daily "lights out" rule at 10 PM, but your siblings stay up until midnight. Talk openly about it. See if you can agree on a mutual plan or meet in the middle. If your new habit can also benefit them, they might be more open to supporting you. For instance, if you decide on a cleaning habit, that might make the shared areas tidier for everyone.

21. Checking In With Yourself

Once a week or once every two weeks, ask yourself how the new habit is going. Are you following it most days? Do you feel bored? Is it helping your life in the way you hoped? If it is not working, you might need to tweak it. That could mean doing it at a different time of day or making the action smaller. If it is going well, you can think about adding another good habit or increasing the challenge slightly.

---

22. Handling Emotions That Block Habit Building

Sometimes emotions like anxiety or sadness get in the way of good habits. If you feel low, you might skip your daily walk or journaling. The best approach is to have a gentle version of your habit for such days. For example:

- **Normal Version**: 20 minutes of walking.
- **Gentle Version**: 5 minutes of strolling around the block when you feel tired or down.

This gentle version keeps you from quitting altogether. You still keep the pattern of showing up, even if it is a smaller action. Over time, maintaining even a short version can keep your new routine alive until you feel better.

---

23. The Science of Habit Loops

Research says that when you repeat a behavior enough times, certain pathways in your brain strengthen. It is like creating a well-worn path through a forest. Each time you do the action, you walk the path again, making it a bit clearer. Eventually, it is easy to follow that path without much thought. This is why repetition matters so much in building habits. The more often you do it, the less mental effort it takes.

But remember, a few missed days do not erase the path entirely. It does weaken it a bit, which is why it is best to get back on track soon. The more consistent you are, the stronger the habit pathway becomes.

24. Balancing Your Routine

When you add habits, keep an eye on your daily schedule. If you pack too many routines into your day, you might feel overwhelmed. Balance is key. If your day is already full, choose habits that fit well with what you are doing, or remove something less important to make space. For instance, if you want to practice guitar but spend an hour scrolling on your phone each night, you might cut down that phone time to 30 minutes and use the extra half-hour to practice.

---

25. Planning for the Long Run

Building a habit is not just about changing your behavior for a week or a month; it is about creating a positive pattern that can stay with you for years. Think of each new habit as part of your long-term plan. Maybe you want to be healthier in the next 5 years, or you want to improve your skills. Each good habit you set now can make that future easier. Instead of waiting for some big life event to push you, you begin the change step by step.

Closing Thoughts on Building Good Habits

Good habits are like anchors in daily life. They hold you steady when motivation goes up and down. They also reduce decision fatigue by making helpful actions automatic. By starting small, linking habits to existing routines, and providing yourself with regular rewards, you can set patterns that last. Over time, these habits will support your health, your goals, and your overall view of yourself as someone who can learn, grow, and stick to what matters.

In the next chapter, we will look at how to handle fear. Fear often stops people from trying new habits or stepping out of their comfort zone. Learning to manage fear can help you put in place all the good routines you have been planning. By seeing fear for what it is and using practical steps, you can move forward with more confidence and less worry, giving your new habits the best chance to thrive.

CHAPTER 14: OVERCOMING FEAR

Fear is a strong emotion that can keep you from doing things that might be good for you. It can also protect you from danger, which is its helpful side. The problem arises when fear becomes so large it blocks you from positive growth or from taking healthy risks. In this chapter, we will look at what fear is, why it forms, and ways to handle it so it does not rule your life. By learning simple methods to face and reduce fear, you open up more possibilities in areas like work, relationships, and personal goals.

---

1. What Fear Really Is

Fear is a natural response your body and mind create when they sense a threat. Long ago, this was crucial for survival—if a wild animal appeared, fear made your heart beat faster and gave you energy to run or defend yourself. Today, threats are often less about animals and more about social or personal risks, such as fear of failing a test or fear of being judged.

Even though the threats are different, the body can react in similar ways: racing heartbeat, tense muscles, and fast breathing. This reaction can be helpful if the fear is real and immediate (like jumping back from a moving car). But if the fear is about a challenge that could help you grow—like speaking up in class—then letting that fear stop you can be harmful in the long run.

---

2. Common Types of Fear

People fear many things, but here are a few common examples:

- **Fear of Failure**: Worrying that you will mess up and look bad. This can lead to avoiding activities or challenges entirely.
- **Fear of Rejection**: Scared someone might say no to your request or not like your ideas. This can keep you from asking for help or sharing your opinion.

- **Fear of the Unknown**: Uncertainty about the future can make you freeze and not move forward with plans.
- **Fear of Making Mistakes**: Being so scared of doing something imperfectly that you never begin at all.
- **Fear of Discomfort**: Not wanting to experience any anxiety, sweat, or stress, so you avoid tasks that might have a short period of discomfort but lead to growth.

Recognizing which type of fear affects you can help you find the right approach to handle it.

---

3. How Fear Grows

Fear often grows bigger when we repeatedly avoid the thing that scares us. For instance, if you fear public speaking, each time you turn down a chance to speak, your mind learns that "speaking is dangerous." This reinforces the fear. Over time, something that might have been mildly scary becomes huge in your mind because you have never faced it.

Also, negative self-talk can make fear worse. If you tell yourself, "I will definitely fail," or "Everyone will laugh at me," you feed the anxiety. This can create a loop: fear leads to avoidance, avoidance leads to more fear, and so on.

---

4. The Benefits of Facing Fear

Facing fear does not mean never feeling scared again. It means learning to do what matters even when nervous. Some benefits include:

1. **Growth in Confidence**: Each time you face a scary task, you prove to yourself that you can handle more than you thought.
2. **New Opportunities**: Many interesting things in life (like meeting new friends or trying a new skill) involve a bit of risk. Overcoming fear opens those doors.

3. **Less Regret**: If you always let fear stop you, you may look back later and wish you had tried. Pushing past fear can reduce that regret.
4. **Less Power for the Fear**: When you face it, you learn that even if things do not go perfectly, you can handle the outcome. This shrinks the fear's hold over you.

---

5. Small Steps vs. Giant Leaps

One of the best ways to handle fear is gradual exposure. Instead of jumping into your biggest terror all at once, take smaller steps. For example, if you are afraid of speaking in front of a large group, start by:

- **Speaking in front of a friend or two** about a short topic.
- **Joining a small study group** and giving a mini-presentation.
- **Volunteering to speak up with a short statement in class or at a club meeting.**
- **Gradually moving to bigger audiences** as your comfort grows.

Each step can still feel nervous, but it is more manageable than leaping straight to a huge audience. Over time, your mind learns that speaking publicly is not as bad as it once seemed.

---

6. Replacing Fearful Thoughts

When you catch yourself thinking fearful thoughts like "I can't do this," you can challenge them with more balanced thoughts. You might say, "I feel scared, but I've handled challenges before, so maybe I can handle this too." You are not lying to yourself; you are reminding yourself there is more than one way to see the situation.

Other helpful thoughts could be:

- "Making a mistake does not mean I'm a failure."
- "This might be tough, but I can grow from trying."
- "I can ask for help if I get stuck."

Over time, these more balanced thoughts can cut down the power of the negative ones.

7. Physical Techniques to Calm Fear

Because fear affects your body, learning simple physical steps can help:

1. **Deep Breathing**: Slow, deep breaths can send signals to your brain that you are safe. Try a simple count of 4 seconds breathing in, hold for 1 second, then 4 seconds breathing out.
2. **Muscle Release**: Tighten your muscles for a few seconds, then let go. Start with your toes and move up to your head. This can ease overall tension.
3. **Posture Shift**: Stand or sit upright, roll your shoulders back, and hold your head up. This position can help you feel more balanced and less helpless.
4. **Slow Movements**: If you are shaking or fidgeting, deliberately slow your movements. This can trick your brain into feeling calmer.

8. Visualizing Success

Some people find it helpful to picture themselves doing the scary thing successfully before they actually do it. For instance, if you are afraid of giving a speech, close your eyes and imagine yourself speaking clearly and calmly, with the audience listening. See yourself finishing and feeling proud. This mental exercise can reduce the shock of the real event, as your mind has rehearsed a positive outcome.

9. Support from Others

You do not have to face fear alone. You can:

- **Talk to a Trusted Person**: Share your worries with someone who can listen and offer encouragement.
- **Seek a Mentor**: If your fear is related to a skill (like writing or sports), find someone who does it well. They might share tips or guide you through first steps.
- **Form or Join a Group**: Many people have fears about similar things. A group can allow you to practice together. For instance, a public speaking club can give you a safe environment to try short talks.
- **Professional Help**: If fear is very strong, a counselor or therapist can teach specific methods to work through it.

Knowing others are on your side can make a huge difference in feeling brave enough to act.

---

10. Learning from Failure or Mistakes

One big reason people stay stuck in fear is they assume if they fail, it proves they are not capable. But mistakes do not define your worth. They are simply part of learning. When you make an error, ask:

1. **What went wrong?** Maybe you tried to speak too fast or forgot to prepare enough.
2. **What can I do better next time?** This might be making an outline or practicing more.
3. **What did I do well?** Even in a mistake, there can be good points. Maybe you tried a new technique or had the courage to begin in the first place.

By focusing on lessons, you turn an unpleasant moment into growth rather than letting it become a reason to hide.

---

11. The Power of Self-Talk

Your inner voice can be a supporter or a bully. If it says, "You'll look silly," you might freeze. If it says, "You can manage this if you take it slow," you gain the courage to move forward. Being aware of your self-talk is crucial. When you notice a harsh comment in your mind, replace it with a gentler statement. Over time, this repeated practice can shift your mindset toward one that is more open to challenges.

12. Facing Fear in Different Areas of Life

- **School or Work**: You might fear asking questions, giving presentations, or trying for a new position. Practice in low-pressure settings, then step up to bigger challenges.
- **Relationships**: You might fear being honest with friends or family. Start by sharing a small concern. If the reaction is respectful, move on to bigger issues.
- **Personal Goals**: You might fear failing at a hobby or project. Begin with small tasks and let yourself learn from errors.
- **Social Situations**: Fear of being judged in a crowd is common. Try going with a friend to a small event, then try a bigger event when you feel ready.

13. Recognizing When Fear Is Helpful

Not all fear is bad. If you feel a strong sense of dread around a specific situation, ask if there is a real danger. For instance, if you fear walking alone at night in an unsafe area, that might be a sign to take precautions. Fear that warns you of actual harm is protective. The trick is to tell the difference between helpful caution and fear that is overblown or based on unrealistic ideas.

14. Dealing with Anxiety That Feels Overwhelming

Sometimes fear is more than just a single worry; it can show up as intense anxiety. Signs of high anxiety might include strong panic, racing thoughts, or physical responses like a pounding heart that does not ease. If anxiety is very strong, it can help to:

- **Pause and Breathe**: Focus on slow, long breaths.
- **Ground Yourself**: Name five things you can see, four you can touch, three you can hear, two you can smell, and one you can taste. This brings you back to the present moment.
- **Seek Professional Support**: Therapists or doctors can offer techniques or treatments to manage persistent anxiety.
- **Use Self-Soothing**: Engage in calming activities, like gently washing your face with warm water, listening to soft music, or hugging a pillow to feel more secure.

15. When Fear Holds You Back from Building Good Habits

In Chapter 13, we covered how to build good habits. Fear can sabotage this process if you are afraid of trying a new routine or worried that you will fail. Sometimes you might avoid starting because you think, "What if I can't keep it up?" The best approach is to begin small and allow mistakes. Show yourself that a slip is not the end. Over time, your confidence grows as you see yourself continuing even with bumps along the way.

16. Setting Manageable Goals to Overcome Fear

If you have a fear of driving, for example, you can set a goal to drive around a quiet block once a day for a week. Then progress to a busier street for the next week. By slowly raising the challenge, you reduce the shock to your system. Each success, no matter how small, signals to your brain that you can face the fear and come out okay.

17. Seeing Fear as a Signal

In some cases, fear can act like a sign that tells you an event is important. If you feel scared to audition for a play, it might mean you care about acting and want to do well. Rather than seeing that fear as a block, see it as proof that you care. Turn that care into planning or practice so that you are better prepared for the big moment. When you let fear remind you to prepare, it becomes a helpful tool rather than just a wall holding you back.

---

18. Interrupting the Fear Cycle

Fear often follows a pattern: a thought arrives ("What if I fail?"), and your body reacts with stress symptoms. Then you might interpret those symptoms as confirmation that the situation is scary. To break this cycle:

1. **Label It**: When the fearful thought comes, name it: "This is my fear of failure talking."
2. **Question It**: Ask, "Is there real evidence that I will fail?" or "Could I handle it even if it goes badly?"
3. **Change the Narrative**: Replace it with, "I might succeed or might learn something. Either way, I can handle the outcome."
4. **Act Anyway**: Take a small step forward, like a test run or a practice session.

By not letting the cycle run unchecked, you reduce its hold.

---

19. Rewarding Courage

Overcoming fear, even a tiny bit, is an act of bravery. You can reward yourself by acknowledging it:

- **Write Down a Moment of Bravery**: Keep a journal. Each time you do something despite being scared, note it. Read these entries later when you need a reminder of your strength.

- **Share with Someone Trustworthy**: Tell a friend or family member, "I was scared to do this, but I did it anyway." Getting a thumbs-up can reinforce your progress.
- **Allow a Simple Treat**: This can be a small break, a relaxing bath, or a mild sweet snack if that feels right to you. Keep it modest so it does not become an unhealthy pattern, but do let yourself feel proud.

---

20. Patience with the Process

Facing fear is rarely a quick fix. It is a process that may include steps backward at times. One day you might feel brave enough to speak up in a group, and the next day you might feel scared again. That does not erase your progress. It is just part of human nature to have ups and downs. Keep reminding yourself that building confidence can be like learning a new language: it takes practice, time, and patience.

---

21. Fear vs. Caution

It is worth repeating that being fearless does not mean ignoring common sense. You should still look both ways before crossing the street. You should still prepare well before trying a new activity. Caution involves wise steps to reduce real risk, while fear often magnifies the risk in your mind to a point where you avoid doing things that are safe enough with proper care.

---

22. Helping Friends or Family Who Are Fearful

If you see someone else held back by fear, you can help by:

- **Listening**: Let them share what they feel without judgment.
- **Encouraging Small Steps**: Suggest a small step they can handle and cheer them on.

- **Offering Practical Help**: Maybe they are afraid to go to an event alone. Offer to go with them.
- **Sharing Your Story**: If you overcame a fear, explain how you did it and what you learned. Sometimes knowing others have faced fears helps them feel less alone.

But do not force them to face fears they are not ready to tackle. Everyone has their own pace.

23. Checking Your Progress

After some time trying to overcome a specific fear, look back and see how far you have come:

- **Compare Old You to Now**: Maybe before, you could not even think about the activity without panic. Now you can talk about it more calmly.
- **Note Any Wins**: Even if you have not completely removed the fear, stepping forward in small ways is a real gain.
- **Adjust if Needed**: If you feel stuck, change your approach. Maybe you need more help, smaller steps, or a different kind of practice.

24. Building a Long-Term Mindset

When you make facing fear a habit, you build a new mindset. You start to believe, "I can do things that seem scary if I plan, practice, and allow myself to feel a bit of anxiety." This can spill over into all parts of life. For example, if you gain confidence in speaking up in a club, you might later feel braver about asking for a raise at your job or traveling to a new place alone.

25. Bringing it All Together

Fear can protect you from true harm, but it can also keep you from trying new and possibly great experiences. By identifying your type of fear, challenging scary thoughts, and taking small steps forward, you train yourself to move past it. It takes time, patience, and sometimes help from others, but each small act of courage adds up. Overcoming fear is not about never being scared again; it is about not letting that feeling control what you do with your life.

When you can manage fear, you free yourself to build good habits, chase meaningful goals, and interact more openly with the people around you. You also grow a sense of pride in your ability to face what once made you freeze. As you continue exploring ways to improve your self-respect and personal growth, remember that fear is just one feeling among many. You have the power to guide it, shape it, or lessen its effects by steady practice and a belief in your own resilience.

Chapter 14 Summary

- **Fear is a normal reaction to possible dangers, but it can grow too large and block positive actions.**
- **Common fears include fear of failure, fear of rejection, and fear of the unknown.**
- **Avoiding a scary thing often makes fear bigger over time. Facing it in small steps can weaken its grip.**
- **You can replace fearful thoughts with more balanced ones, reminding yourself you can manage challenges.**
- **Physical actions like deep breathing or muscle release can calm the body.**
- **Visualizing success and seeking help from friends or mentors can boost courage.**
- **Mistakes are chances to learn, not proof of personal failure.**
- **Pay attention to your inner voice and change harsh words into supportive ones.**

- Some fear is useful if it keeps you safe, but too much can stop healthy growth.
- Overcoming fear is a process that involves patience, small steps, and sometimes professional guidance.
- Rewarding small acts of bravery can encourage more steps forward.
- You can help others face fear by listening, offering small challenges, and being supportive.
- By reducing fear, you make room for building better habits and chasing bigger goals.

With fear in a healthier place, you can apply the strategies from earlier chapters—like setting realistic goals, breaking old habits, and building new routines—more effectively. Fear will not be a constant blocker. Instead, you can recognize it, learn from it when it is helpful, and move past it when it is not. This skill will help you in the remaining chapters, where we will continue to look at ways to build a kinder approach to yourself and to make choices that align with your long-term well-being.

CHAPTER 15: THE IMPORTANCE OF FORGIVENESS

Forgiveness is a concept that many people talk about, but not everyone finds easy to apply. It is often linked to letting go of anger toward someone who has hurt you. But it also involves releasing feelings of blame you might hold against yourself. By learning to forgive, you free up mental and emotional space that can be used for better things. This does not mean forgetting what happened or saying it was okay. It simply means not letting the hurt control your life any longer. In this chapter, we will explore why forgiveness matters for your well-being, common obstacles that make it hard, and practical methods to develop a forgiving mindset. Each section will focus on everyday language and real tips you can use, even if you find the idea of forgiveness uncomfortable right now.

---

1. Understanding What Forgiveness Is (and Is Not)

Many people think that to forgive someone, they have to approve of what they did. That is not correct. Forgiving does not mean you think the bad act was acceptable. It does not mean you must stay close to the person who hurt you, either. It simply means releasing the resentment that can eat away at your peace.

- **Not Approval**: Forgiveness does not say, "What you did is fine." It says, "I will not carry this anger forever."
- **Not Weakness**: Choosing to forgive can require strength. You are refusing to allow the harmful act to define you.
- **Not Instantly Trusting**: If someone broke your trust, you can forgive but still maintain healthy boundaries. Trust and forgiveness are not the same.
- **Not Always Reconciliation**: Sometimes, the person who hurt you might not be safe to be around. You can still let go of resentment in your heart while keeping distance for your own protection.

These differences matter because some people are afraid to forgive. They think it will force them to pretend everything is okay or go back to a harmful relationship. But in reality, you can forgive internally without letting yourself be mistreated again.

2. Why Forgiveness Matters

1. **Reduces Emotional Weight**
   Holding grudges can drain your energy. Thoughts of anger or revenge might pop up, making it hard to enjoy life. By forgiving, you lessen that load. This can help you feel lighter and more focused on positive goals.
2. **Improves Mental Health**
   Resentment can feed stress and sadness. Over time, it can turn into ongoing anger that affects how you see yourself and others. Studies show that forgiving attitudes can support better emotional balance.
3. **Supports Physical Health**
   Chronic anger may lead to problems like high blood pressure or trouble sleeping. Letting go of anger might help you relax, rest better, and face daily tasks with more energy.
4. **Helps You Move Forward**
   Without forgiveness, you may stay stuck in a painful past. You could keep replaying the event that hurt you, never fully focusing on the present. When you forgive, you can step into new experiences without carrying the same bitterness.
5. **Fosters Better Relationships**
   In families or friendships, learning to forgive can improve how people interact. That does not mean you let others walk all over you. It just means you break the cycle of resentment and hurt.

3. The Two Sides of Forgiveness: Others and Yourself

Forgiveness can go in two main directions:

- **Forgiving Others**: This involves releasing anger toward someone who caused you harm or disappointment.
- **Forgiving Yourself**: This means letting go of guilt or shame you feel for mistakes you made. Many people find self-forgiveness even harder than forgiving others because they feel they must punish themselves.

Both are important. If you cannot forgive yourself, you might struggle to feel worthy of good things in life. If you cannot forgive others, you might stay locked in cycles of blame. Balancing these two forms of forgiveness often leads to a healthier sense of personal worth.

---

4. Why It Can Be Hard to Forgive

1. **Fear of Being Hurt Again**
   People might cling to anger because they believe it shields them from more pain. If they stay angry, they will not let the offender get close. But that anger can also push away healthy connections.
2. **Feeling That It Lets the Other Person Off**
   There is a common idea that forgiveness means the other person does not face consequences. But remember, you can forgive internally while still allowing fair consequences to happen if needed (like legal action or setting boundaries).
3. **Deep Wounds**
   If the harm done was very serious—like betrayal by a close friend—letting go can feel impossible. Deep wounds might require more time and possibly professional help before you can release that bitterness.
4. **Cultural or Family Influences**
   Some environments promote holding on to grudges as a show of strength. People might say you are "soft" if you let go. Understanding that true strength often involves learning to handle anger in a balanced way can help you move past such influences.
5. **Lack of Tools**
   Sometimes, people just do not know how to start the forgiveness process. They might want to let go but have no idea what steps to take.

5. Common Myths About Forgiveness

- **Myth: Forgiveness Requires Confrontation**
  Some assume you must speak directly to the person and say "I forgive you." While that can happen, it is not required. Forgiveness can be purely internal.
- **Myth: You Must Forget the Event**
  Even if you forgive, the memory may remain. The difference is that the memory no longer has the same emotional grip on you.
- **Myth: You Have to Rush It**
  Some people feel pressure to forgive right away. Real forgiveness may take time, especially if the hurt was large. Going too fast might lead to "fake" forgiveness, where you pretend to let go but still feel bitterness.
- **Myth: Forgiveness Solves Everything**
  Though it can help you move on, there might still be consequences. Healing can take work in other areas, like trust-building or therapy, especially if there was severe harm.

6. Steps Toward Forgiving Others

Forgiveness is often described as a process rather than a single moment. Here is one approach:

1. **Acknowledge the Hurt**
   You cannot forgive what you refuse to admit. If someone harmed you, be honest about how it affected you. Write it down or talk to a trusted friend or counselor.
2. **Feel Your Emotions**
   It is important to allow yourself to be upset, sad, or angry about the harm. Ignoring these emotions can make them linger. Facing them can be tough, but it is a step toward letting them go.
3. **Consider the Other Side (If Safe to Do So)**
   This does not mean excusing the harm. But sometimes,

understanding that a person acted out of ignorance or their own pain can lessen the intensity of your anger. Be careful here—if what they did was truly abusive, you do not need to justify it.

4. **Decide to Let It Go**
   This is the core of forgiveness. You make a choice to not let the wrongdoing be the main event in your mind. You do not keep replaying it or plotting revenge.
5. **Follow Through**
   Each time the memory comes up with anger, remind yourself of your choice. You might say internally, "I am letting this go. I choose not to carry this resentment."
6. **Set Boundaries if Needed**
   Forgiving does not mean allowing the same harm again. If the person is untrustworthy, you can keep a healthy distance or have rules for how you interact. Forgiveness is about freeing your inner feelings, not ignoring reality.

---

7. The Power of Self-Forgiveness

Some people find it simpler to forgive a friend than to forgive themselves. You might blame yourself for past choices, or you might think you are not worthy of kindness because of something you did.

1. **Acknowledge the Mistake**
   Just like with forgiving others, you need to be honest about what happened. Pretending it did not occur only drags out the self-blame in subtle ways.
2. **Accept Responsibility**
   If you did something wrong, own it. That may include apologizing if your actions hurt someone else, or making repairs where possible.
3. **Learn the Lesson**
   What did this mistake teach you? Perhaps you learned you need to be more careful with words or more thoughtful with money. Taking the lesson to heart can reduce the urge to keep punishing yourself.
4. **Speak Kindly to Yourself**
   Try not to call yourself cruel names in your mind. Ask how you would

talk to a close friend who made the same error. Chances are, you would be gentler with them than you are with yourself. Aim for that same level of understanding for your own slip-ups.

5. **Make a Plan to Improve**
Self-forgiveness does not mean you shrug and say, "No big deal." You can commit to doing better. This sense of progress can help you move forward without lingering shame.

---

8. Golden Gems: Deeper Insights on Forgiveness

1. **Forgiveness Has Layers**
Sometimes, you think you have forgiven, only for an old feeling to pop up months later. This can happen as you grow and see the event in new ways. It does not mean you failed at forgiving. It means you are peeling back more layers of emotion and letting them go at a deeper level.

2. **Anger Can Hide Other Feelings**
Anger is sometimes easier to feel than sadness or humiliation. If you find it tough to forgive, examine if you are masking a deeper hurt. Recognizing deeper emotions can be the key to genuine release.

3. **Forgiving vs. "Stuffing Down" Emotions**
Some people misunderstand forgiveness and just push negative emotions away, hoping they vanish. True forgiveness involves facing them, dealing with them, and then choosing to move on.

4. **You Can Forgive Even If the Person Does Not Apologize**
Waiting for an apology might keep you stuck. The act of forgiveness is about your heart, not their admission of guilt.

5. **It Can Help Even If the Person Is Gone**
You can forgive someone who has moved away or even passed on. You do not need them present or aware of your choice for it to help your emotional freedom.

9. Tools to Start the Forgiveness Process

1. **Journaling**
   Write a letter to the person who hurt you. Say everything you would like to say, but do not send it. This is for your own processing. You can then choose whether to keep or destroy it.
2. **Guided Visualization**
   Some people find it useful to imagine themselves talking to the person in a safe setting. They might picture themselves setting down a heavy burden and walking away feeling lighter.
3. **Support Groups or Counseling**
   Talking to others who have gone through similar experiences can normalize your feelings. Professional counselors are trained to guide you through these steps without pushing you too hard.
4. **Specific Rituals**
   Some find closure in small personal activities. For example, writing down the painful event on a piece of paper and then tearing it up or tossing it in water, as a symbol of release.
5. **Daily Reminders**
   Place a short note where you can see it, something like, "Today, I choose to let go of harmful anger." Simple visuals can keep you on track.

---

10. When Forgiveness is Most Challenging

Some hurts feel nearly impossible to forgive. This can be the case with deep betrayals, long-term harm, or events that changed your life forever. In these situations, it is normal to feel stuck for a long time. You might need extra help from mental health professionals, supportive friends, or spiritual leaders if that suits you. Healing might come slowly. That is okay. The main thing is not to rush yourself or feel guilty if you are not ready. Over time, you may find layers of anger softening, especially if you actively work through it.

11. Forgiveness in Day-to-Day Life

Not all forgiveness tasks are giant issues. Sometimes, daily annoyances can build up. If a coworker makes a rude remark or a family member forgets your birthday, you might carry small resentments. Practicing quick forgiveness on these smaller problems can strengthen your ability to handle bigger hurts. Think of it like exercise: letting go of small frustrations is like doing regular mental push-ups that keep your emotional health strong.

12. Balancing Forgiveness and Boundaries

Sometimes people worry that if they forgive, they will lose their sense of boundaries. However, the two can coexist:

- **Forgiveness**: You choose not to hold anger.
- **Boundaries**: You decide how you will interact with someone who may still act harmfully.

If a friend repeatedly borrows money and never pays back, you might forgive them for the past. But you can still decide not to lend them money again. This is not about revenge; it is a practical step to avoid repeating the negative cycle.

13. Signs You Are on the Path of Forgiveness

- **Less Intense Emotions**: You notice you do not feel as much anger when you think of the event.
- **Less Need for Revenge**: You do not find yourself fantasizing about ways to get back at the person.
- **Neutral Thoughts**: You can recall the incident with a calmer mindset, more like a fact than a fresh wound.
- **Gradual Release of Tension**: You feel physically more at ease; your shoulders might not tense up when the topic arises.

- **Sense of Freedom**: You are more focused on your current life and not stuck in the past.

14. Forgiving vs. Rebuilding Trust

One tricky area is trust. If a friend broke your trust, you might wonder if forgiving them means you must let them back into your life in the same way. This is not always required. Rebuilding trust is a separate process that usually involves consistent honest behavior over time. You can forgive someone but still decide that your relationship will be at a different level, or you might not have a relationship at all. That choice depends on the situation and whether the person has shown real change.

15. Forgiveness and Apologies

An apology from the person who hurt you can help the forgiveness process. It shows they recognize the harm and possibly want to fix it. However, not everyone will apologize. Some might not see their wrongdoing, or they might be too stubborn or lost in their own world. If you base forgiveness on them admitting fault, you may never find peace. So it can help to see their apology as a bonus rather than a requirement. Your inner healing does not have to wait on their actions.

16. Self-Forgiveness Techniques for Deep Shame

When people carry shame for something big they did—like causing harm to someone they cared about—they can spiral into constant self-punishment. Here are some methods that can help:

1. **Identify What You Can Repair**: If there is a way to apologize or offer some kind of amends, do so. This does not erase the past but shows genuine remorse.

2. **Learn Healthier Behaviors**: If your actions came from a lack of coping skills, work on building better ways to handle stress or anger. This might involve therapy, books, or group programs.
3. **Practice Self-Compassion**: Gently remind yourself that being human involves making mistakes. The key is to grow from them, not let them define you forever.
4. **Seek Professional Help if Needed**: If the shame runs very deep, a counselor can help you break it down. They are trained to guide you without harsh judgment.

---

17. Helping Children Understand Forgiveness

If there are children in your life—maybe as a parent, older sibling, or teacher—you can model forgiveness in small ways. When they upset you, calmly explain why their behavior was not okay, but also show them that your love or care continues. Teach them to say sorry when they make mistakes, and gently encourage them to accept apologies from others. By learning the basics of forgiveness early, children can grow into adults who handle conflicts with more kindness and less grudge-holding.

---

18. Handling Forgiveness When the Person Repeats Harm

A special challenge arises when the individual who hurt you keeps doing it. This might be an unkind relative, a friend who gossips about you, or a partner who continues the same destructive habits. You might forgive once, but what if it happens again and again?

- **Recognize Patterns**: If the person shows a repeated pattern, you can forgive emotionally but might need stronger boundaries or even a complete break from them.
- **Avoid Naive Trust**: Forgiveness does not mean believing their promises blindly. Watch if their actions match their words.

- **Protect Yourself**: If the repeated harm is severe or abusive, focus on your safety. Forgiveness in your heart can come later, but your well-being is a priority.

---

19. Forgiveness in a Larger Context

Sometimes the person who hurt you is part of a bigger system, like a workplace or a social group. Forgiveness in these cases might involve understanding that certain structures or cultures encouraged harmful acts. You might also realize that multiple factors led to the event. This does not reduce the harm but might help you see it is not purely personal. Recognizing external factors can help you let go of the idea that everything was targeted at you. It might also inspire you to work toward changes in those systems, if possible.

---

20. Making Forgiveness a Personal Value

For many people, forgiveness is not just a one-time act—it becomes part of who they are. That does not mean they never feel anger or never set boundaries. Instead, they develop a forgiving mindset that helps them handle conflicts or hurtful events with more calm. This approach can reduce stress over a lifetime and lead to healthier connections. However, it is also possible to forgive selectively, based on each situation. Not everyone is ready or willing to adopt forgiveness as a central life principle. That choice is personal.

---

21. Checking if You Are Forcing Forgiveness

Sometimes, families or communities push people to say, "I forgive you," even when they do not feel ready. Forced forgiveness may look polite but can lead to hidden resentment. If you feel pressured to forgive before you are prepared, it might help to slow down. Tell those pushing you that you need time to process. It is healthier to work through emotions so you can arrive at real forgiveness rather than a show of it.

22. Real-Life Example of Forgiving a Friend

Imagine you had a friend who revealed one of your secrets to others. You felt embarrassed, and your trust was shaken. At first, you might be furious. Over time, you decide to see why they did it. Maybe they were trying to seem interesting to someone else or had poor judgment in that moment. You let yourself feel the hurt, talk to another trusted friend or a counselor about it, and then choose to let go of the resentment. You do not pretend the event never happened, but you decide not to let it define your future or your sense of worth.

Does that mean you trust them with secrets again? Maybe not right away. You might keep certain private details to yourself until they earn back your trust. But you no longer hold a burning grudge each time you see them. You have forgiven, though you remain cautious about sharing personal info with that friend. This is a balanced approach to forgiveness and boundaries in everyday life.

23. Activities to Practice Forgiveness

1. **Gratitude List**
   Sometimes focusing on what you have, rather than what you lost, can shift your mindset. If you are stuck in anger, listing things you appreciate in your life can broaden your outlook.
2. **Mindful Breathing**
   Sit quietly and take slow breaths. As you exhale, imagine releasing angry or bitter thoughts. This can be done a few minutes each day.
3. **Forgiveness Journal**
   Keep a small notebook where you write any negative emotions or resentments that come up. Note why you felt that way, then add a line about what letting go might look like.

4. **Story Rewrite**
   Write the "story" of the hurtful event. Then rewrite it from a perspective of learning or growth. This does not mean lying about it, but focusing on what you can do differently moving forward.
5. **Volunteer or Help Others**
   Doing good deeds for others can sometimes soften the hardness we feel from anger. When you are in a helpful mood, resentment might feel less pressing.

---

24. The Ongoing Nature of Forgiveness

Keep in mind that forgiveness often is not a single decision that solves everything forever. You might have to reaffirm that choice many times. Each time the memory of the hurt resurfaces, you may need to remind yourself: "I've decided not to let this own my thoughts." Over weeks, months, or years, it usually gets easier. The important thing is that you are taking steps that free you from being locked in the past.

---

25. Wrapping Up: Forgiveness as a Tool for Growth

Forgiveness is not about waving away the wrong that happened. It is about choosing freedom over chains of bitterness. It allows you to put your energy into what benefits you, rather than into maintaining grudges. Real forgiveness takes honesty (with yourself about the hurt), time (to process the emotions), and effort (to practice release). But the payoff includes less stress, clearer thinking, and a more open heart toward new experiences and people.

By building a forgiving mindset—both toward others and yourself—you strengthen your ability to navigate life's challenges with less emotional baggage. This can lead to better mental well-being, stronger relationships, and an overall sense of calm. As you continue your path of personal growth, keep forgiveness in mind as a powerful tool. It might not fix everything, but it can remove big roadblocks to your happiness.

CHAPTER 16: FINDING HOPE IN HARD TIMES

Hard times happen to everyone. They can include losing a job, coping with a health crisis, dealing with family trouble, or feeling uncertain about the future. During these moments, hope can feel distant. You may wonder if things will ever get better. Yet hope is important for getting through challenges. It keeps you moving when life feels heavy. This chapter will explore what hope means, why it can slip away, and methods to rebuild it. We will also look at practical steps to help you handle sadness or hopelessness, so you can keep going even when life feels harsh.

---

1. Defining Hope in Everyday Terms

Hope is the feeling or belief that positive outcomes are still possible, even if you cannot see them right now. It is not blind optimism where you deny problems exist. Instead, it is the steady sense that you can find a path forward, or that life can get better with effort, patience, or changes in your surroundings.

- **Realistic Hope**: You acknowledge challenges but also see potential solutions or small rays of light.
- **Maintaining Perspective**: You may say, "I do not know how, but I believe there could be a way through this."
- **Action-Oriented**: Hope often leads to looking for steps you can take, no matter how tiny.

---

2. Why Hope Can Disappear

When life hits you with multiple problems at once, or a single huge crisis, hope might fade. Common reasons include:

1. **Overwhelming Stress**
   Prolonged stress can wear down your emotional strength. You may reach a point where you feel you have nothing left to give.
2. **Repeated Disappointment**
   If you have tried solutions that failed again and again, you might think nothing will ever work.
3. **Isolation**
   Feeling alone or lacking support can make it hard to believe in a better future.
4. **Internal Critic**
   Negative self-talk can convince you that you are doomed to fail or that you are unworthy of improvement.
5. **Lack of Clear Paths**
   Sometimes you cannot see any options, which makes it feel like you are trapped in a dark corner.

---

3. Why Hope Matters

Without hope, motivation often drops. You may quit trying to solve problems or ignore your emotional needs. Over time, this can lead to deeper sadness or even despair. Holding on to hope, however small, can help you:

- **Stay Motivated**: You keep working toward solutions.
- **See Creative Options**: A hopeful outlook opens your mind to ideas you might miss if you believe all is lost.
- **Better Handle Stress**: Hope gives you emotional fuel. If you believe there might be a light later, you can handle the dark moments more calmly.
- **Find Strength in Connections**: Hope often encourages you to reach out to others for help, which can bring fresh support or resources.

---

4. The Connection Between Hope and Resilience

Resilience is the ability to bounce back after hardship. Hope is closely tied to resilience because it propels you to keep going, even when events turn bleak. A resilient person may still feel sadness or worry, but they keep a small inner flame that says, "I can keep trying." This synergy between hope and resilience can help you adapt, learn, and grow from difficulties instead of being crushed by them.

5. Myths About Hope

- **Myth: Hope Is Only for the Optimistic**
  People who are usually serious or cautious can still foster hope. It does not require a bubbly personality.
- **Myth: Hope Means Ignoring Problems**
  Genuine hope does not hide from reality. It faces challenges while believing in the possibility of better outcomes.
- **Myth: If You Have Hope, You Will Never Feel Down**
  Hopeful people still have low moments. The difference is they do not stay in hopeless mode forever.
- **Myth: Hope Is Always Grand**
  Hope can be small and personal, like hoping to sleep better tonight or hoping to mend a fight with a friend.

6. Methods to Find Hope During Hard Times

1. **Focus on Small Wins**
   Look for little things that went right today. Even if it is just finishing a single chore, note it as a sign that not everything is stuck.
2. **Create Short-Term Goals**
   When the future looks daunting, set a mini-goal for today or this week. Achieving something small can boost your morale and remind you that progress is possible.
3. **Seek Out Support**
   Share your situation with someone who cares. They might offer comfort or new ideas. Feeling connected can restore some optimism.
4. **Limit Constant Negative Input**
   If you are always watching upsetting news or scrolling through

stressful media, your mind can get stuck in doom. Try to balance that with upbeat or educational content.
5. **Use Imagery**
Some people like to picture themselves successfully dealing with their current challenge. This mental rehearsal can plant seeds of possibility.

---

7. Handling Feelings of Hopelessness

When hopelessness kicks in, you might feel numb or stuck. Here are steps to cope:

1. **Name It**
Recognize that you are experiencing a powerful emotion. Saying "I feel hopeless right now" can be the first step to dealing with it.
2. **Separate Feelings from Facts**
Emotions are valid, but they might not be accurate reflections of reality. Just because you feel hopeless does not mean the situation truly has no solutions.
3. **Practice Self-Care**
This could be taking a warm shower, drinking water, or resting. Caring for your basic needs can lift your mood enough to see small possibilities again.
4. **Seek Help Immediately if You Feel Unsafe**
If hopelessness leads to thoughts of harming yourself or giving up on life, call a trusted person or a help line. Professional help can be crucial during severe emotional crises.
5. **Remind Yourself of Past Victories**
Think of a time you overcame a problem before. This can spark the idea that you might overcome again.

---

8. Golden Gems: New Ways to Spark Hope

1. **Hope Mapping**
Draw a simple map of your life events, marking challenges you have

162

faced and how you got through them. Seeing past solutions can fuel belief in future solutions.

2. **Learning from Role Models**
Study stories of people who overcame hard problems. Note how they found a path forward. This can shift your thinking from "It's impossible" to "Maybe I can do something too."

3. **Micro-Hobbies**
Start a tiny hobby that gives immediate small gains, like planting a seed in a cup. Watching it sprout can be a physical reminder that growth happens slowly but surely.

4. **Hope Journal**
Each day, write one line about what you would like to see happen in the next month. It can be very simple, like, "I want to feel calmer." Over time, you accumulate a list of positive directions for your mind.

9. The Role of Faith or Belief Systems

For some people, religious or spiritual faith can be a powerful source of hope. They believe in a higher power or in the idea that events can serve a greater purpose. Others might find hope in human connections, nature, or personal values. The key is not which system you follow, but how you draw optimism and comfort from it. If you do have a belief system, engaging in its practices—like meditation, prayer, or community gatherings—can provide an anchor during storms.

10. Balancing Acceptance of Reality with Hope

You may wonder how to stay hopeful if things are truly bad, such as a terminal illness or a large debt. Balancing acceptance and hope means acknowledging the facts while still seeking areas where you can act. For example, a person with a chronic illness might accept that it is life-altering but still hope for pain management or improved daily routines. Or someone in debt might accept they cannot fix it overnight but hope to create a plan to slowly recover financially. This blend of realism and optimism is often the most stable way to hold on to hope without denying the truth.

11. Hope in Relationships

When relationships suffer—due to fighting, distance, or misunderstandings—hope might fade. You may think the bond cannot be repaired. Here is how hope can help:

- **Try Small Repairs**: Send a kind note or share a gentle apology. Little acts can open a door for healing.
- **Offer Second Chances Carefully**: Hope does not mean ignoring red flags, but it can involve giving a loved one room to make amends or show improvement.
- **Look for Shared Interests**: If things have been sour, doing a simple enjoyable activity together can remind you of why you care about each other.
- **Seek Mediation**: Sometimes a neutral party can help find common ground. This can rekindle hope in a strained relationship.

12. Hope in Wider Communities

At times, society faces problems such as natural disasters, economic downturns, or conflicts. It can be easy to feel there is no point in trying to help. But remember that many positive changes have started with a few people who kept believing things could improve. You do not have to fix everything alone. Joining or supporting community groups that work on solutions can renew your sense of hope. Even if the results come slowly, taking part can give you a sense of purpose.

13. Misplaced Hope vs. Realistic Hope

Not all hope is equal. Sometimes, people cling to false promises or impossible outcomes. This can lead to bigger disappointment. Realistic hope is grounded in what can reasonably happen, even if it is a stretch. For instance, hoping to become a top athlete in a week is not realistic. But hoping to learn a new skill over a few months with practice is more plausible. Balancing your aims with facts helps keep hope from turning into self-deception. That said, do not confuse a big dream with an impossible dream. Many achievements seemed impossible until someone put in enough effort or found a new approach.

14. Handling Critics Who Dismiss Hope

You might meet people who say hope is naive. They might tell you to face reality and give up. Remember:

- **They May Be Projecting Their Own Doubts**: Perhaps they once tried to fix a problem and failed, so they assume everyone else will fail too.
- **You Can Still Be Honest and Hopeful**: You do not have to hide the truth of a bad situation. You can name it and still seek possible ways to improve it.
- **It Is Your Life**: You decide whether to keep looking for a path forward. Critics do not live your life or face your hardships as you do.

15. Hope and Personal Growth

Periods of struggle can lead to unexpected personal growth. When you work through hard times, you may discover new strengths or skills. You might become more patient, more empathetic, or more courageous. This does not mean the struggle was good, but it shows that even in negative conditions, positive changes can arise. Keeping a hopeful viewpoint helps you notice and develop these changes, turning setbacks into stepping stones for personal development.

16. Building Hope Through Daily Rituals

1. **Morning Thought**
   Upon waking, think of one thing you are looking forward to that day, even if it is small like having a nice cup of tea.
2. **Evening Reflection**
   Before bed, note one thing that went better than expected or one sign of improvement. This keeps your mind from dwelling only on what went wrong.
3. **Affirmation or Mantra**
   Have a short phrase like, "Better days can come," or "I can grow from challenges." Repeat it when stress rises.
4. **Physical Symbol**
   Some keep a small token—like a smooth rock or a piece of string—reminding them of hope. Touching it can bring a moment of calm in a bad day.

---

17. Seeking Professional Support for Hopelessness

Sometimes, no matter what you try, a cloud of hopelessness lingers. This might be linked to depression or anxiety conditions that need more than self-help steps. In these cases, reaching out to a mental health professional is wise. Therapists and counselors are trained to help you explore underlying issues, challenge unhelpful thinking, and develop coping plans. Medication might also be an option if a doctor finds that it could help you stabilize your mood. Seeking professional help is not a sign of weakness; it is a sign that you value your well-being enough to get expert support.

---

18. Encouraging Hope in Others

If you see someone close to you losing hope, you can:

- **Listen Without Judging**: Sometimes, people need to vent their fears or sadness. Let them speak without jumping in with advice right away.

- **Offer Concrete Help**: If they are stuck, maybe you can help with small tasks or guide them to resources. Practical support can spark hope more than empty words.
- **Share Success Stories**: Remind them of times they succeeded in the past or share stories of others who overcame similar problems.
- **Be Patient**: You cannot force someone to feel hopeful. Offer steady support rather than pushing them to cheer up instantly.

---

19. Overcoming Setbacks in Hope

You might have a bit of hope, try something, and then face another obstacle. This can feel crushing. But setbacks are common in any process of improvement. Consider these steps:

1. **Allow Sadness for a Moment**
   Acknowledge you are disappointed. That is normal.
2. **Reassess**
   Did you aim too high too fast? Did you miss a resource you could use? Adjust your plan if needed.
3. **Seek Another Angle**
   Sometimes you just need a different strategy or more time. Keep your eyes open for new ideas.
4. **Remind Yourself of the Bigger Picture**
   One setback does not erase all progress. Look at the total path you have followed. You might still be closer to a solution than you were before.

---

20. Linking Hope to Gratitude

Focusing on what is still good in your life, even during troubles, can keep hope alive. Gratitude and hope often feed each other. When you notice positive aspects—a supportive friend, a kind act from a stranger, or a skill you still have—hope can grow because you see evidence that not everything is dark. This does not mean ignoring problems. It just means you also recognize the bright spots. This balanced viewpoint can power you through tough days.

---

21. Hope in the Face of Long-Term Problems

What if you are dealing with a long-term issue, like chronic illness, ongoing financial struggles, or repeated social conflicts? Hope might weaken after many tries. In these cases:

- **Break It Down**: Focus on short intervals, like one day at a time.
- **Adjust Goals**: Maybe your big dream has to be trimmed into smaller achievable steps that can bring partial relief or improvement.
- **Find Community**: Groups of people who share similar issues can provide understanding and mutual aid. You might find encouragement from those who have walked a similar path.
- **Celebrate Tiny Gains**: Not every improvement is huge, but small ones add up. Even better self-care or lighter pain for a short period is worth recognizing.

---

22. Embracing Change for Renewed Hope

Sometimes hope requires accepting that life will not look exactly as you wanted. For instance, you might realize a certain career path is no longer possible, or a relationship cannot be restored to its old form. This acceptance can be painful, but it can open the door to new possibilities. Letting go of the old dream can free you to see new options. Over time, you may find hope in fresh directions you never considered before.

---

23. Creative Outlets to Build Hope

When words are not enough, you can turn to creative activities:

- **Art**: Paint, draw, or make collages that represent your feelings. Seeing them on paper can help you process them.
- **Music**: Singing or playing an instrument can release tension and bring a sense of achievement.
- **Writing Stories**: Turning your struggles into short fiction might give you a sense of control over the narrative. You can also imagine hopeful endings.
- **Movement**: Simple dance or even walking while noticing nature can shift your mood. Physical action often refreshes the mind.

Creativity can serve as a way to express fears and begin seeing new angles, thus strengthening your sense of hope.

---

24. Real-Life Example: Finding Hope After a Major Loss

Imagine a person named Alex who lost their job unexpectedly. Their sense of security was shaken, and they felt hopeless about finding something else. At first, Alex spent days feeling stuck and alone, focusing on all the worst outcomes. Then a friend suggested they reach out to a career center. Alex agreed, mostly out of desperation. The career counselor helped them update their resume and practice interviewing. They also joined a support group for people seeking new roles.

In that group, Alex heard others' stories of losing and finding new work. This sparked a tiny spark of hope: maybe it was not over. Alex applied for various positions and faced rejection at first, but each interview sharpened their skills. Over a couple of months, Alex landed a decent job in a related field. The job was not exactly the same as their old one, but it provided enough stability and a new start. Through this process, Alex discovered that hope did not remove all challenges, but it provided the energy to keep trying and eventually find a path forward.

25. Concluding Thoughts on Hope

Hope is not a magical fix that erases problems instantly. It is more like a steady light that helps you see there might be a door or a window in what looks like a solid wall. Hard times can be draining, and feeling low is normal when life is difficult. But even a small amount of hope can make a big difference. It encourages you to keep searching, to accept help, and to believe in a future that might be better than today's situation.

By practicing small steps—like focusing on short-term goals, seeking support, and caring for yourself—you nurture hope in a real, down-to-earth way. Over time, this hopeful mindset can become part of your inner foundation. You will still face obstacles, but you will have a mental toolbox to handle them, reminding you that improvement, growth, or unexpected solutions can still arise. Embracing realistic hope keeps you connected to life's potential and helps you take daily actions that may, little by little, lead to brighter days.

CHAPTER 17: DAILY ACTIONS FOR GROWTH

All the advice so far in this book can feel large if you only see it as big changes. But real growth often takes place in small, everyday moments. These daily moments can shape how you see yourself and what you believe you can do. This chapter will explore how simple daily actions can help you feel good about yourself and keep making progress. It will also cover how to stay consistent and handle days when you do not feel motivated.

1. Why Daily Routines Matter

A daily action is something you do each day, no matter how small. When people think of self-improvement, they might picture a huge goal, like running a marathon or writing a big novel. Those goals are fine, but the real engine of growth is usually in the small steps you take each day. Here is why:

1. **Steady Progress**
   If you do a small helpful action every day, you will see growth over time. Even a short exercise routine each morning adds up to many hours of movement in a year.
2. **Less Stress**
   Trying to make a huge change all at once can be overwhelming. Smaller actions are easier to handle, so you are less likely to give up in frustration.
3. **Clear Focus**
   A daily routine gives you a clear direction. You do not have to wonder, "What should I do today to feel better about myself?" You already have a plan of small tasks that support your well-being.
4. **Builds Self-Trust**
   When you follow a simple plan each day, you prove to yourself that you can stick to a promise. This trust in your own word can improve how you see yourself.

2. Choosing a Small Daily Action

Daily actions will look different for each person. You should pick something that fits your life and your current needs. For instance:

- If you want to feel calmer, you might choose to do 5 minutes of quiet breathing after you wake up.
- If you want to feel more confident, you might write down a quick note each evening about one thing you did well that day.
- If you want to improve your focus, you might read a few pages of a non-fiction book each afternoon.

The point is to find an action that links to the part of yourself you want to strengthen. It does not have to be long or complicated. Aim for something that takes only a few minutes, if that helps you stay consistent.

3. Connecting Daily Actions to Your Values

In Chapter 10, we talked about personal values. A powerful way to build daily actions is to connect them to those values. For example:

- **If you value kindness**, you might choose one act each day to help someone or send a caring message.
- **If you value learning**, you can plan to watch a short video or read a short article on a topic you want to understand better.
- **If you value health**, you can make a habit of going for a 15-minute walk after dinner.

When your action matches your value, you will be more motivated to do it. It will not feel like just another task on your list. Instead, it becomes a way to honor what is important to you.

4. Examples of Simple Daily Actions

1. **Morning Gratitude Note**: Keep a small notebook by your bed. Write one thing you are thankful for when you wake up.
2. **Set a Daily Intention**: Each morning, decide on a simple mindset for the day, like "I will be patient" or "I will learn something new."
3. **Check Your Schedule**: Look at your day's tasks first thing in the morning. This helps you feel prepared and reduces sudden stress.
4. **Hydration Habit**: Drink a glass of water before each meal. This supports health and reminds you to stay hydrated.
5. **Mini Cleanup**: Pick a small area (like your desk or a corner of your room) to tidy for 2 minutes. A neat space can help clear your mind.
6. **Quick Movement**: Do a simple stretch or walk up and down your stairs a few times. This can wake your body up.
7. **Encourage Someone**: Send a short text or say a kind word to a friend, family member, or coworker each day.
8. **Short Reflection at Night**: Before sleeping, note something that went right or something you learned.

---

5. Fitting Actions into Your Day

To avoid forgetting your daily action, connect it to something you already do (this idea is sometimes called "habit stacking"). For example:

- Right after you brush your teeth in the morning, you do your 2-minute stretch.
- The moment you sit down at your desk at work, you write one line about your goal for the day.
- Right before you eat lunch, you drink a full glass of water.

By linking new actions to existing routines, it becomes easier to remember them. You do not have to rely on willpower or memory as much because the old routine triggers the new one.

6. Making Daily Actions Enjoyable

One key to keeping a daily habit is to make it pleasant or meaningful. If an action feels like a chore, you might stop doing it. Here are a few ways to add enjoyment:

1. **Add Music**: If your action is cleaning a corner of your room, play a favorite song while you do it.
2. **Track Progress Visually**: Put a checkmark on a calendar each day you do your task. Watching those marks grow can be fun.
3. **Reward Yourself**: It does not have to be a big prize. Maybe after a week of doing your daily action, you treat yourself to a small break or a simple snack.
4. **Share It**: Tell a friend about your action. Talk about your progress. Feeling connected can make the habit less lonely.

---

7. Handling Days You Slip Up

No matter how well you plan, there might be days when you forget or do not feel up to your daily task. This is normal. Here is how to deal with slip-ups:

1. **Do Not Judge Yourself Harshly**: Missing one day (or even a few days) does not undo all the good you have done.
2. **Ask Why It Happened**: Were you too tired, busy, or stressed? Did you simply forget? Understanding the reason can help you fix the issue.
3. **Make a Simple Adjustment**: If you are too tired at night to do the task, try doing it earlier. If you keep forgetting, set an alarm on your phone.
4. **Keep Going**: The most important thing is to return to your routine the next day. Do not let a slip become a permanent stop.

8. Combining Multiple Daily Actions

You can have more than one daily action if you find that works for you. However, it is often wise to start with just one or two. Once they feel natural, you can add another. For example, you might start by writing a short gratitude note each morning. After a month, if that is going well, you add a midday stretch break. This gradual approach keeps you from feeling overwhelmed.

---

9. Daily Actions for Emotional Health

Emotional well-being can benefit a lot from steady small practices. A few examples:

- **Calm Breathing**: Take a minute or two each day to breathe slowly. Inhale for four counts, pause for one, exhale for four counts. This helps your mind settle.
- **Journaling Feelings**: Write down how you feel once a day. This helps you track changes in mood and spot patterns of stress.
- **Positive Self-Talk**: Each day, say one kind phrase to yourself in the mirror, like "I am allowed to learn and grow."

These daily emotional habits can reduce stress and help you cope better with big challenges.

---

10. Physical Health Actions

Physical well-being also matters. You can pick simple daily tasks that support your body:

1. **Mini Exercise**: If you are new to working out, do 5 push-ups or 10 squats each morning. Over time, you can add more if you want.
2. **Healthy Food Choice**: Decide on one meal each day where you will add an extra serving of vegetables or fruit.

3. **Standing Breaks**: If you sit a lot, stand up every hour and walk around for a minute. This can help blood flow and prevent stiffness.

Remember, these are just examples. You can adjust them to your level and interests.

---

11. Social Connections

Connecting with others can improve your sense of belonging and self-respect. A small daily action might be:

- **Sending a Thoughtful Message**: Text or email a friend to check in or share a kind word.
- **Giving a Genuine Compliment**: At school or work, say something positive to a classmate or coworker, like "Your idea was really helpful."
- **Listening Carefully**: Take a few minutes each day to practice active listening with a friend or family member who wants to talk about their day.

These acts help you feel linked to the people around you, which supports a healthy sense of self-worth.

---

12. Managing Time for Daily Actions

People often say they do not have time for self-care or small routines. Yet many of us spend time on social media, TV, or other activities. This is not a criticism—relaxation is good. But if you feel you cannot fit in a 5-minute routine, you might want to see where your time goes. Consider these tips:

1. **Set a Timer**: If your action is only 5 minutes, use a timer to stay on track. You might be surprised how short 5 minutes feels once you get started.

2. **Choose the Best Part of the Day**: If mornings are rushed, maybe do your small action in the afternoon. If you have more quiet time in the evening, schedule it then.
3. **Replace a Less Helpful Activity**: If you usually scroll on your phone for 15 minutes before bed, do your daily action for the first 5, then scroll for 10 if you still want to.

---

13. Mindset Tips for Daily Growth

A big part of daily actions is your mindset. You can help yourself stick to routines by adopting these views:

1. **It All Counts**: Even if you only manage a tiny bit, it is better than nothing.
2. **Growth Is Ongoing**: Do not look for perfection. Look for steady gains.
3. **Every Day Is a New Start**: If yesterday was rough, today you can do your habit again.
4. **Self-Encouragement**: Speak kindly to yourself about your efforts. A bit of self-support can go a long way.

---

14. Using Tools and Reminders

Many tools can help you remember your daily tasks:

- **Phone Alarms**: Set one for the time you want to do your action.
- **Apps**: Some apps let you check off habits each day and send you friendly reminders.
- **Calendars**: Whether paper or digital, mark each day you complete your task.
- **Sticky Notes**: Put them where you will see them, like on your bathroom mirror or computer.

These simple reminders reduce the mental load of having to keep track on your own.

15. Checking Progress Weekly or Monthly

While your daily action might take a few minutes each day, it helps to step back every week or month and check how it is going. You can ask yourself:

- **Have I done it most days?**
- **Do I feel any improvements—less stress, more skill, better mood?**
- **Is the task still working for me, or do I need to change it?**
- **Is it time to add another small habit or adjust the one I have?**

This reflection ensures you do not keep a habit that no longer helps you. It also lets you see how far you have come, which can boost motivation.

16. Adapting Daily Actions to Life Changes

Life is not static. You might move, start a new job, or face an unexpected event. During these changes, keep your daily action flexible. For example, if your routine is to do a short walk in your neighborhood but you travel for a week, switch to a simple stretching routine in your hotel room. The key is to keep the spirit of the habit alive, even if the details shift.

17. Keeping a Positive Approach

Sometimes, people treat daily actions like a strict chore. If you miss a day, they feel guilty or angry at themselves. But a gentle, positive approach works better:

1. **Use Encouraging Words**: Talk to yourself like a friend would. Instead of saying, "I am useless for missing my workout," say, "I had a busy day, but I can do it tomorrow."
2. **Enjoy the Process**: If you pick actions that truly matter to you, you will naturally like doing them more.

3. **Thank Yourself**: Give a little mental "thank you" to yourself after completing your daily action. This can build a sense of appreciation for your own effort.

18. Overcoming Common Barriers

- **Lack of Motivation**: If you do not feel like doing your action, remind yourself of your reason. Is it tied to a value you hold dear? Or maybe you can do a smaller version, like 2 minutes instead of 5.
- **Stressful Days**: If a day is full of problems, do your action as a grounding moment. Even a short break can give your mind some relief.
- **Criticism from Others**: If people around you mock your small routine or say it is pointless, remember you are doing it for your own growth, not to please them.

19. Seeing Daily Actions as Self-Care

Self-care is not always bubble baths or spa days. It can be these tiny routines that keep you stable and positive. By caring for your body, your mind, or your relationships in small ways, you show yourself that you matter. This can deepen your self-acceptance because you begin to see yourself as someone worthy of kind actions—even if they are brief.

20. Building a "Daily Action Menu"

If you like variety, you can create a "menu" of tiny tasks. Each morning, pick one item from the menu. For example:

1. Write a short note of encouragement to a friend.
2. Read two pages of a book.
3. Do 10 squats.

4. Organize one drawer.
5. Spend 3 minutes thinking about what you want out of the day.
6. Practice writing down one positive thing about yourself.

Having a menu means you can choose what feels right that day. This approach works well for people who get bored doing the same thing daily but still want structure.

---

21. Connecting Daily Actions to Larger Goals

Small actions can be stepping stones to a bigger dream. Suppose your goal is to write a book someday. Your daily action might be writing 100 words every evening. Over time, you will accumulate many words without the stress of trying to do it all at once. Or if you hope to run a race, your daily action might be a quick jog around the block. By linking these small tasks to a bigger picture, you keep your motivation high because you see how each day's effort fits into a grander scheme.

---

22. Balancing Multiple Areas of Life

You might want to grow in different parts of life—health, relationships, learning, and so on. It is okay to have daily actions that cover different areas, but do not overload yourself. You could have a short physical action, a short mental or emotional action, and a short social action each day. Example:

1. **Physical**: 10 minutes of easy exercise.
2. **Emotional**: Write a short reflection about your feelings.
3. **Social**: Send a check-in message to a friend or relative.

This spread can be beneficial, but if it feels like too much, pick one area and focus there first.

23. Teaching Daily Actions to Younger People

If you have younger siblings or children in your life, you can show them the power of a daily routine. It can be something simple like reading 5 minutes before bed or saying one thing they liked about their day at dinner. Teaching kids the idea of small, steady steps helps them handle tasks and stress in a more confident way. They also learn that growth is not a huge, sudden leap but a slow build over time.

24. Sharing Your Daily Actions

Sometimes, telling a friend or joining an online group where people share daily habits can keep you inspired. Reading about what others do each day might spark new ideas for you. Also, having someone cheer you on or ask you about your progress can keep you on track. But be careful not to compare your progress to others in a negative way. Remember, each person's life is unique.

25. Final Thoughts on Daily Growth

Daily actions are like seeds. They might be small, but given time and care, they grow into strong habits and positive changes in how you see yourself. By choosing just a few minutes of focused effort each day, you can shape your mood, your relationships, and your confidence. Over weeks and months, these small acts add up to noticeable growth. And on the days when life feels tough, you can rely on these small routines to ground you. You do not have to do everything at once; you just have to keep going, bit by bit.

In the next chapter, we will look at learning from mistakes. Mistakes are a natural part of life, but many people feel ashamed when they happen. We will discuss how to turn errors into lessons rather than letting them harm your sense of worth. Combined with the daily steps you are taking, a healthy view of mistakes can free you to take more chances and trust yourself more deeply.

CHAPTER 18: LEARNING FROM MISTAKES

Everyone makes mistakes. It is one of the most basic truths about being human. Yet many people feel deep shame or try to hide when they mess up. They may think a mistake means they are not good enough or that they never learn. This chapter focuses on how mistakes can actually help you grow. We will look at ways to respond to errors in a healthier way and how to find lessons in them. You will learn that making mistakes does not have to damage your self-esteem—it can strengthen it, if you handle the aftermath in a calm, honest manner.

1. Why Mistakes Are Normal

Mistakes happen for many reasons: lack of knowledge, feeling rushed, or simply trying something new. No matter how well you plan, there can always be a slip or unexpected factor. This is part of learning. Think of a baby who is first learning to walk. They fall down many times before they can walk steadily. Nobody sees those falls as failures. They are part of the process.

As adults, we sometimes forget that we are still learning. We might think we should already know how to do everything perfectly. This belief is unrealistic. Even experts in a field continue to make errors—they just use them to improve.

2. Unhealthy Responses to Mistakes

When you respond negatively to your own errors, it can lower your sense of worth. Common negative responses include:

1. **Harsh Self-Blame**: Calling yourself "stupid" or "useless" because of one slip.
2. **Hiding or Lying**: Pretending nothing happened or covering it up out of fear of judgment.

3. **Quitting Completely**: If you fail once, deciding you are never trying again.
4. **Getting Defensive**: Lashing out at others who point out the mistake, instead of looking at the facts.

These reactions can turn a small mistake into a bigger problem. They also block you from learning anything beneficial.

---

3. Healthier Ways to View Mistakes

Instead of seeing errors as proof of your lack of worth, try viewing them as information. A mistake tells you something about what does not work or what you still need to learn. It can guide you to a better path if you allow it. Here are some healthier ways to view mistakes:

- **A Step in Discovery**: Each mistake can show you a step in finding the right approach. Think of it like a puzzle piece, helping you see how something does or does not fit.
- **Proof You Are Trying**: People who never make mistakes often are not trying new things. If you made an error, it means you had the courage to try.
- **A Call to Slow Down**: Mistakes can remind you to breathe, check details, or ask for help. They can prevent bigger problems down the road.

---

4. Breaking Down a Mistake

When an error happens, you can process it by asking these questions:

1. **What Happened?**
   Get clear on the facts. What was supposed to happen, and what actually happened?
2. **Why Did It Occur?**
   Were you missing some skill? Did you rush? Was there a misunderstanding with someone else?

3. **How Do I Feel About It?**
   Are you angry, sad, or embarrassed? Acknowledging these feelings helps you handle them better.
4. **What Can I Learn?**
   Is there a skill to practice, a routine to fix, or a communication step you missed?
5. **What Will I Do Next Time?**
   Based on what you learned, decide on a new approach or a better plan.

This method transforms a mistake into a lesson. You actively look for ways to improve. Over time, you become less afraid of messing up because you see that you can handle the outcome productively.

---

5. Apologizing and Making Amends

Some mistakes affect other people's feelings or property. In such cases, part of learning is to apologize or fix what you can. This might involve:

- **Saying Sorry**: A simple, sincere apology without excuses can help repair trust.
- **Offering to Correct**: If possible, fix the damage. Maybe that means replacing something or giving back time.
- **Explaining, Not Excusing**: You can briefly explain why the mistake happened, but do not make it sound like you are shifting blame or ignoring responsibility.

Apologizing does not make you weak. It can show maturity. It also signals to others (and yourself) that you are accountable for your actions.

---

6. Overcoming Shame After a Mistake

Shame is the feeling that "I am bad" rather than "I did something bad." It is deeper than guilt. To beat this feeling, remember:

1. **Focus on the Action, Not Your Identity**: Making an error does not define your entire character. You remain a person with many traits—some strong, some in progress.
2. **Talk to Someone You Trust**: Sharing the story with a friend or counselor can help you see it more clearly. They might point out that you are too hard on yourself.
3. **Practice Self-Kindness**: Speak to yourself the way you would speak to a loved one. If you would forgive a friend, why not forgive yourself?

---

7. Learning from Mistakes in Relationships

Arguments and misunderstandings happen in friendships and families. Sometimes you might say something hurtful by accident. Instead of hiding, it helps to:

- **Admit the Error Right Away**: Do not let resentment grow.
- **Listen to the Other Person**: Hear out how they felt. This can prevent repeating the mistake.
- **Change the Behavior**: Saying sorry is important, but showing you will not do it again is equally important.

These steps can turn a conflict into a lesson that strengthens a bond rather than breaking it.

---

8. School and Work Mistakes

In school or at work, mistakes can seem huge because you might fear bad grades or losing a job. But remember:

1. **Feedback Is Helpful**: If a teacher or boss points out your error, treat it as guidance. Ask questions if you are not sure how to fix it next time.
2. **Monitor Your Stress**: High stress can lead to more errors. Try to pace yourself and stay organized.

3. **Practice**: If you keep messing up in the same area, find a way to practice more. Seek extra resources or a mentor.

Mistakes in these settings can be stepping stones toward becoming better at what you do—if you take them as clues for improvement.

---

9. Fear of Repeating the Mistake

Sometimes, after making an error, you might feel scared to try again because you do not want to fail twice. This fear can freeze progress. To handle it:

1. **Improve Your Approach**: Check what specifically went wrong last time. Adjust your method so you are not just repeating the same steps blindly.
2. **Try a Smaller Scale**: If you made a mistake on a big project, test your new plan on a smaller version to gain confidence.
3. **Remember: Mistakes Happen**: Even if you fail a second time, you can still learn. Each attempt gives you more data on what works and what does not.

---

10. Turning Mistakes into Growth

Here is a short process to convert an error into personal development:

1. **Calm Down**: If you are upset, take a breath or walk away for a moment. A calm mind thinks more clearly.
2. **Reflect**: Use the "What happened, why, how do I feel, what can I learn" questions.
3. **Formulate a New Strategy**: Create a plan to fix or avoid the same mistake.
4. **Take Action**: Test your new strategy in a real situation.
5. **Share What You Learned**: Talk to a friend or coworker about your experience. Teaching someone else can also solidify your learning.

This loop of reflection and action helps you become more flexible and resilient over time.

11. Dealing with Mistakes You Cannot Fix

Some errors have lasting effects that cannot be undone—like saying harsh words to a person who then moves away, or missing a big deadline that cannot be extended. If you cannot fix it:

1. **Find a Way to Make Peace**: Accept that you cannot change the past. This is not about letting yourself off the hook, but about moving forward instead of remaining stuck.
2. **Learn the Deeper Lesson**: Ask if there is a bigger takeaway. Maybe you learn the importance of speaking kindly because words can leave a long-term mark.
3. **Channel Regret into Action**: Use the regret to motivate better behavior in the future. For instance, if you missed an important chance, you might become more organized to avoid it next time.

12. Mistakes from Miscommunication

Sometimes mistakes happen because two people did not understand each other correctly. If you think a problem came from unclear messages:

- **Double-Check**: Ask the other person to repeat what they heard. Make sure it matches what you meant.
- **Write It Down**: In important tasks, put details in writing to avoid confusion.
- **Stay Patient**: People have different ways of understanding. Patience can prevent small misunderstandings from becoming big issues.

Learning better communication can reduce many avoidable errors in the future.

13. Handling Criticism

When you make a mistake, you might face criticism from others. Criticism can be tough on self-esteem. But there are ways to handle it better:

1. **Listen for the Useful Part**: Sometimes criticism points out something you did not notice. Even if the tone is harsh, try to pick out any valid points.
2. **Stay Calm**: Getting defensive or angry may block you from learning. If you need a moment to cool off, take it.
3. **Ignore Excess Cruelty**: If the person is just insulting you, and not offering real feedback, do not let it tear you down. Their approach might be about their own issues.
4. **Ask for Suggestions**: If the critic does not offer ways to fix the problem, ask politely, "How do you think I could do better next time?" This can shift the talk from blame to solutions.

---

14. Teaching Yourself to Handle Errors Calmly

If you are used to panicking whenever something goes wrong, you can train yourself to respond more calmly. Here are some ideas:

- **Mental Note**: Say in your mind, "Oops, that did not go as planned. Let's see what's next."
- **Breathe**: A few slow, deep breaths can help your body and mind relax.
- **Positive Reframe**: You might say, "This is a chance to learn."
- **Small Pause**: If possible, take a short break to gather your thoughts before trying to fix the mistake.

---

15. Role Models Who Learned from Mistakes

Look at stories of famous inventors, artists, or leaders. Many faced repeated failures before they found success. For example, writers often have their manuscripts rejected many times before a publisher says yes. Inventors might produce dozens of prototypes that fail before one works. These stories remind us that mistakes and success often travel together.

16. Group Mistakes and Shared Responsibility

Sometimes a mistake involves a team—maybe a group project at school or a work project with coworkers. In such cases:

1. **Share Responsibility**: Do not point fingers at each other. Figure out where the system broke. Perhaps no one double-checked the final details.
2. **Brainstorm Fixes Together**: Each person might have a piece of the puzzle on how to avoid the problem next time.
3. **Stay Respectful**: Blaming can destroy trust. A respectful talk about what went wrong can unite the group to solve future issues.

17. Applauding Effort over Perfection

A mistake often shows you tried something that was not easy. If you only ever do what you already know perfectly, you will not grow much. By focusing on effort instead of perfection, you create a safer mental space to explore new things. You might say:

- "I'm proud I gave it a shot, even though I stumbled."
- "The outcome was not perfect, but I see what I learned."

This attitude can lower the fear of trying and build your courage to keep going.

18. When Others Won't Let Go of Your Mistake

Sometimes, people around you keep bringing up an old error, making it hard for you to move on. In that situation:

- **Acknowledge It Once**: You can say, "I did mess up, and I've learned from it. I've taken steps to do better."
- **Set Boundaries**: If they keep bringing it up in a hurtful way, it is fair to say, "I understand you're upset, but I need us to focus on the present now."
- **Prove by Actions**: Over time, consistent good behavior can show that you are not repeating the same mistake. They might need to see this before they fully trust you again.

---

19. Teaching Kids About Mistakes

If you have younger siblings, children, or students, you can help them see errors as normal. Praise them when they try a new skill, even if they fail at first. Avoid punishing them harshly for honest mistakes. Instead, help them understand what went wrong and how they can improve. This approach builds resilience and a willingness to keep learning.

---

20. Self-Forgiveness After Big Errors

In Chapter 15, we touched on forgiveness. That includes forgiving yourself when you make a serious mistake. You might experience strong regret or guilt. Follow steps like:

- **Accept Responsibility**: Acknowledge the full scope of what happened.
- **Apologize If Needed**: If others were harmed, reach out in a sincere, respectful way.
- **Learn and Change**: Show real effort to avoid repeating the error.
- **Release the Shame**: Shame only keeps you stuck. Recognize that everyone is flawed, and you can still strive to be better each day.

21. Turning Mistakes into Strengths

Occasionally, the solution you find after a mistake becomes a unique strength. For instance, maybe you typed the wrong code in a computer program, but while fixing it, you discovered a new, better way to structure your code. Or perhaps you forgot to bring a dish to a potluck, so you quickly invented a simple recipe from ingredients on hand, and it became everyone's favorite. Mistakes can lead to unexpected creativity if you remain open-minded.

22. Keeping a "Mistake Log"

If you want to see clear growth over time, you can keep a brief "mistake log." Write:

- **What the mistake was**
- **Why it happened**
- **What you learned**
- **How you will prevent it next time**

Reviewing your log occasionally can remind you of how you have improved. It also shows that errors can be stepping stones, not roadblocks. Just be sure you keep the tone of the log friendly and helpful, not punishing.

23. Sharing Lessons with Others

When you are comfortable talking about your mistakes, you can help others avoid the same pitfalls. This might be as simple as telling a younger relative, "Hey, I tried that once, and here's what went wrong. Maybe you can do it differently." You do not have to present yourself as perfect. In fact, people often trust someone who admits they have messed up and learned. It shows honesty and wisdom. Helping others learn from your experience can also make you feel better about the fact you once messed up.

24. Avoiding Repetitive Errors

If you find you make the same mistake over and over, it might signal an underlying issue. Perhaps you have a habit of rushing or not paying attention to details. Or maybe you are afraid to ask for help. In that case:

1. **Identify the Pattern**: Notice which details repeat each time.
2. **Try a Different Tactic**: Doing the same thing again expecting a different result rarely works. Look for a new strategy.
3. **Get Support**: Talk to someone who is good in that area or find a resource like a tutorial, book, or class.
4. **Track Your Steps**: If your actions are scattered, write them down step by step. This can help you spot where you keep going wrong.

25. Conclusion: Mistakes as Your Allies

While mistakes can hurt in the moment, they do not have to ruin your self-image or your path forward. By facing them directly, apologizing when needed, and analyzing what happened, you can turn those moments into valuable lessons. Over time, you may even realize that your biggest steps of growth happened after an error showed you what was missing or broken.

Embracing the idea that mistakes are part of everyday life can free you from perfectionism and constant fear of failing. Instead, you will see yourself as someone capable of learning—someone who can bounce back and do better. This viewpoint supports a stronger sense of self-worth because you no longer tie your value to always being perfect.

In the next chapter, we will explore how to put kindness into practice. Kindness to others, and also kindness to yourself, can expand your self-acceptance and well-being. Combined with what you have learned about daily actions and learning from errors, a mindset of kindness can help you connect with people more honestly and build a caring environment around you.

CHAPTER 19: PUTTING KINDNESS INTO PRACTICE

Kindness is often seen as a simple concept. Yet truly being kind—both to others and yourself—can change the way you see the world. It can uplift your mood, strengthen your relationships, and even boost your sense of worth. In this chapter, we will explore how small, regular acts of kindness can shape your daily life. We will also look at how being kind does not mean ignoring your own needs or letting people step on you. Instead, it involves a balanced approach where you care for yourself while showing warmth toward others.

---

1. Why Kindness Matters for Growth

Kindness is not just about making other people feel good. It also helps you:

1. **Reduce Stress**
   When you act kindly, your body can release certain chemicals that help you feel calmer. Studies show that doing caring acts can lower tension and bring a mild sense of happiness.
2. **Build Self-Respect**
   Each time you choose to be gentle with someone—even yourself—you confirm that you are a caring person. This simple fact can lift your view of who you are.
3. **Improve Relationships**
   People generally respond well to kindness. Even small actions can make others more open, supportive, and willing to listen. This can create a cycle where you treat them well and they treat you well in return.
4. **Create a Healthier Environment**
   Whether at school, work, or home, a little bit of consistent kindness can set a calmer, friendlier tone. Over time, others might mirror your example, and kindness can spread.

5. **Encourage Personal Growth**
   Being kind often involves empathy—imagining what someone else feels. This empathy can help you learn patience, understanding, and better ways to communicate.

---

2. What Real Kindness Looks Like

Some people see kindness as giving expensive gifts or making big gestures. While that can be part of it, true kindness often comes from the small, daily ways you show you care. Examples include:

- **Listening Attentively**: When a friend talks about their day, you focus on their words rather than checking your phone or thinking about your own problems.
- **Offering Genuine Help**: This could be helping a neighbor with groceries, or guiding a classmate who is confused about homework.
- **Using Thoughtful Words**: Complimenting someone's effort, saying "thank you" sincerely, or just telling a person you appreciate them can mean a lot.
- **Sharing What You Have**: It can be small—like a piece of knowledge, a tool, or a spare pen—when someone needs it.
- **Checking In**: Sending a quick message to someone who might be lonely or stressed. A simple "How are you doing?" can show you care.

At the core, kindness is about recognizing another person's worth or need, and acting in a gentle, supportive way.

---

3. Kindness vs. People-Pleasing

It is important to note that being kind is not the same as saying "yes" to everything or letting people treat you poorly. Some people confuse kindness with people-pleasing, where they do whatever others want in order to avoid conflict or gain approval. True kindness comes from a place of warmth and respect for both yourself and others. If an act of "kindness" leads you to feel used or resentful, it might not be genuine kindness. Balancing your own needs with your wish to help is part of being truly caring in a healthy way.

4. Kindness Toward Yourself

Being kind to yourself might sound odd if you are used to putting yourself last. However, treating yourself gently is a key part of growing a positive sense of who you are. Some ways to practice self-kindness include:

1. **Positive Self-Talk**
   Notice how you speak to yourself in your head. Try replacing harsh labels or constant criticism with more fair, calm observations.
2. **Allowing Mistakes**
   As we learned in the previous chapter, errors are normal. Remind yourself that messing up does not make you a bad person. It just means you are learning.
3. **Resting and Relaxing**
   Taking a break when you are tired is a form of self-care. It is not laziness to recharge. Pushing yourself until you burn out can lead to worse outcomes in the long run.
4. **Celebrating Little Wins**
   When you do something good—like finishing a task or helping a friend—pause and recognize it. A simple "good job" to yourself can build your confidence.
5. **Seeking Help When Needed**
   Asking for support is also a kind act toward yourself. It shows you value your well-being enough to let others assist you.

When you treat yourself with kindness, you have more emotional energy to give. It becomes easier to be patient, caring, and present for others.

5. Daily Acts of Kindness for Others

Just like we discussed daily actions for personal growth, you can form a habit of daily kindness. Simple ideas include:

1. **Greeting People Warmly**: Whether it is a neighbor, coworker, or someone you see at the store, a friendly "hello" and a smile can brighten their day.
2. **Writing a Nice Note**: Leave a short compliment for a family member, friend, or teacher. Handwritten notes can feel special in a digital world.
3. **Complimenting Effort, Not Just Results**: Telling a friend, "I admire how hard you worked on this," can mean more than simply praising the final outcome.
4. **Being Polite with Workers**: When you buy something at a store, say "please" and "thank you." Treat service staff with respect—this small kindness can make a big difference.
5. **Offering Your Time**: If someone is overwhelmed, see if you can lighten their load. Maybe you can help carry something, watch their pet for a moment, or give them a quick ride.

---

6. Balancing Boundaries and Kindness

It is possible to be kind without losing your boundaries. Some ways to keep a healthy balance:

1. **Know Your Limits**
   If helping someone means you will be late for an important responsibility, it might be okay to say, "I'm sorry, I can't right now." You can still wish them well or suggest another form of help.
2. **Offer Choices**
   If a friend keeps asking for big favors, you can choose smaller ways to be supportive. For example, if they want you to drive them for hours, you might say, "I can drop you off at the bus stop or help you look up bus times, but I can't drive the whole way."
3. **Recognize Manipulation**
   Some people might misuse your kindness if they see that you never say no. Keep an eye on patterns: if a person only contacts you when they want something, you might need to limit how much you do for them.

4. **Take Care of Your Own Health**
   If you are drained, stressed, or unwell, it is hard to be genuinely kind. Make sure you have the rest and peace you need so that your kindness flows from a healthy place.

7. Why Kindness Helps Relationships

1. **Builds Trust**
   When you consistently act kindly, people sense they can trust you. They know you care about their feelings.
2. **Reduces Conflict**
   Kindness can prevent small problems from escalating. If someone feels respected, they are less likely to become defensive or angry over minor disagreements.
3. **Creates a Positive Cycle**
   One kind act can lead to another. Over time, groups or families can develop a more understanding culture because everyone is contributing small kindnesses.
4. **Helps You Handle Mistakes**
   If you are kind to someone and then later you slip up, they might be more forgiving because they remember how you have treated them kindly in the past.

8. Practical Tips for Being Kind in Hard Situations

1. **Take a Breath Before Reacting**
   In stressful moments—like an argument—pause to breathe. Ask yourself, "How can I respond in a calm way?" This can stop harsh words from flying out.
2. **Practice Empathy**
   If someone is upset, think, "How would I feel in their place?" This does not mean excusing bad behavior, but understanding the root can guide a kinder response.

3. **Use Softer Language**
   Instead of saying, "You're wrong!" you can say, "I see things differently. Can we talk more?" This small shift in tone can maintain peace.
4. **Agree to Disagree**
   Sometimes, kindness means accepting that you do not share the same view but still treating each other with respect.

---

9. Overcoming Barriers to Kindness

Sometimes, negative feelings or past grudges can block you from being kind. If you notice you are holding resentment, think about:

- **Forgiveness** (Chapter 15): Letting go of anger can open space for care.
- **Self-Check**: Ask, "Why am I refusing to be kind here? Am I hurt, angry, or afraid?"
- **Starting Small**: You do not have to force a big gesture. A tiny step can open the door.
- **Seeking Mediation or Support**: In bigger conflicts, a counselor or neutral friend might help you see ways to approach the situation with more compassion.

---

10. Kindness in Different Areas of Life

1. **Kindness at Home**
   Offer to help with chores without being asked, or ask how a family member's day went, really listening to their response.
2. **Kindness at Work or School**
   Support a coworker with a tricky task. Compliment a classmate's presentation. Offer to study with someone who struggles.
3. **Kindness to Strangers**
   Hold the door for someone, give a genuine smile, or pick up litter in a public area. These small acts can make the community feel better.

4. **Kindness in Online Spaces**
   Avoid harsh comments. Respond kindly even when disagreeing. Share helpful resources. A few friendly words can change the tone of a chat or forum.

11. Spreading Kindness Without Bragging

It is natural to feel good about being kind, but constantly announcing your good deeds can come across as seeking approval. Let kindness be its own reward. If others notice, that is a bonus, but do not rely on praise to keep your kindness going. Over time, quiet, consistent acts of caring often gain genuine respect from those who see them.

12. Teaching Kindness to Kids or Younger Siblings

Children learn a lot by watching adults. If you show politeness, empathy, and helpfulness, they will pick up these habits. You can also:

- **Explain Why**: When you do something kind, briefly explain why. For example, "I helped our neighbor carry groceries because it's nice to lend a hand."
- **Praise Their Efforts**: If a child shares a toy with a sibling, say, "That was very thoughtful. How do you think your brother feels now?"
- **Offer Simple Tasks**: Let them hold the door or pass out snacks. Small roles show them they can be kind too.

13. Acts of Kindness Toward Animals and Nature

Kindness is not just for humans. Caring for animals and the environment can grow your sense of empathy. Some simple acts:

- **Feeding Pets Properly**: Making sure your family pet is well-fed, groomed, and played with shows responsibility and kindness.

- **Supporting Wildlife**: If you see an injured bird, gently contact a local wildlife rescue if possible. Or put out a small bowl of water on hot days for passing birds.
- **Recycling and Reusing**: Reducing waste, picking up trash, and using items wisely is kind to the planet. You help keep the environment safer for everyone.
- **Avoiding Harm**: Being careful not to step on insects mindlessly or not throwing harmful substances into nature can reflect a caring attitude.

14. Kindness During Personal Struggle

When you are going through tough times, it might feel hard to care for others. However, even tiny acts of compassion can help you as well:

- **Shifts Your Focus**: By doing something kind, you momentarily step out of your own pain. This can reduce stress and keep you from getting stuck in negative thoughts.
- **Builds Support**: If you help a friend while you are both down, you create a bond. Later, they may return that kindness when you need it most.
- **Shows You Your Strength**: Realizing you can still be kind even when life is not going well is a sign of inner resilience.

15. Avoiding Burnout from Being Too Kind

Yes, there is such a thing as too much giving without rest. If you always put others first and never care for your own needs, you can burn out:

1. **Set Time for Yourself**: Carve out moments in the day just to relax or do what you enjoy.
2. **Know Your Emotional Limit**: If listening to someone's troubles starts wearing you down, it is okay to step back and say you need a short break.

3. **Ask for Reciprocity**: In healthy relationships, kindness flows both ways. If someone constantly takes and never gives, that might be a sign to reevaluate how much energy you invest.
4. **Remember Self-Kindness**: The better you treat yourself, the more genuine your kindness to others can be.

16. Small Group or Community Projects

If you want to extend your kindness beyond individual acts, consider small projects:

- **Organize a Food Drive**: Collect canned goods for a local shelter.
- **Group Cleanup**: Gather friends or neighbors to pick up litter in a park.
- **Support a Fundraiser**: You do not need lots of money. Even sharing the cause or volunteering time can help.
- **Community Share Table**: Some neighborhoods create a free table where people leave unwanted but usable items. Others take what they need and leave what they can.

These collective efforts can boost a sense of unity and help you feel part of something bigger.

17. Handling Negative Reactions to Kindness

Sometimes, you might offer a helping hand, and the person refuses or even reacts rudely. Do not let this discourage you:

- **Stay Polite**: You can calmly say, "No worries," or "I understand," and step back.
- **Respect Their Feelings**: Maybe they prefer independence or have past experiences that make them wary of help.
- **Accept Not Everyone Is Ready**: Your gesture is still meaningful, even if they do not welcome it. Continue being kind in other ways where it is appreciated or helpful.

18. Kindness and Self-Worth

Acting kindly, when done sincerely, can reinforce a positive sense of self. You prove to yourself that you have something good to offer. This can combat feelings of low worth. However, be mindful not to rely solely on helping others as your only source of self-value. Balance is key. You are worthy even on days when you might not be able to help much because you need rest or support yourself.

19. Planning for Consistency

Like other daily actions, being kind can become a habit:

1. **Set a Simple Goal**: Each morning, decide on one kindness you will do. It can be as small as sending a supportive text.
2. **Reflect**: At the end of the day, recall the moment you were kind. How did it feel? This reflection makes the habit stronger.
3. **Mix It Up**: Try different forms of kindness so it does not become mechanical. One day you might help someone with a task, another day you give a compliment, another you share a meal.

20. Dealing with Criticism or Teasing

Sometimes peers might tease you for being "too nice" or "soft." They might act like kindness is uncool. In such cases:

- **Stand Firm in Your Values**: If kindness is important to you, do not let others shame you out of it.
- **Explain Briefly**: You can say, "I think caring is important," or "It feels right for me." You do not owe a lengthy defense if they are not open-minded.

- **Find Like-Minded People**: Spend more time with those who value empathy. Surrounding yourself with supportive people can keep your kindness thriving.

---

21. Random vs. Intentional Acts of Kindness

- **Random Acts**: These are unplanned moments where you see a chance to help—like paying for someone's coffee behind you in line, or picking up something someone dropped. They can be fun and spontaneous.
- **Intentional Acts**: These are planned, like scheduling time to call a lonely relative or deciding you will volunteer for an hour on a certain day. Both types are valuable. Random acts spread small joys, while intentional acts let you go deeper and more steadily.

---

22. Kindness Toward People You Dislike

This can be tricky. You do not have to be best friends with everyone, but showing basic respect and politeness can keep the environment civil. Sometimes, offering a small kindness to a person you have tension with can break ice. For example, if a coworker is often grumpy, politely asking if they need help carrying a heavy box might shift the dynamic slightly. However, be cautious if they truly behave in harmful ways—maintaining safe boundaries is still important.

---

23. Reflecting on Your Kindness Journey

It is helpful every so often to pause and look at how your kindness efforts are going:

1. **Are You Feeling Good Overall?**
   If you are exhausted or resentful, you might need to step back or delegate.

2. **Is It Affecting Your Mood?**
   Do you feel calmer, more open, or happier at times? This can be a sign that your caring approach is benefiting your mental health.
3. **Have Your Relationships Improved?**
   Check if there is less conflict or more trust around you.
4. **Are You Maintaining Self-Kindness?**
   Ensure you are not sacrificing your own well-being in the process.

---

24. Celebrating Kindness

It is okay to recognize and appreciate your kind acts:

- **Write Down Good Moments**: A small journal entry about a kind deed can help you remember that you are capable of generosity.
- **Share Stories with Trusted People**: You can say, "I felt good about helping out today." If they see it as boasting, just clarify you are happy and want to spread positivity, not brag.
- **Enjoy the Ripple Effect**: Sometimes your kind act inspires someone else to do something caring. Knowing you helped create a chain of kindness is a wonderful feeling.

---

25. Final Thoughts on Practicing Kindness

Kindness is not about being perfect or pleasing everyone. It is about consistently choosing to care in little ways, even when it would be easier to be rude or ignore others' needs. By mixing kindness to others with kindness to yourself, you build a balanced sense of self-worth and a more supportive environment. Whether you give a small daily act of compassion or help in a larger way, you are contributing to a world where warmth and understanding can grow.

As you cultivate this practice of kindness—while maintaining personal boundaries and self-care—you will likely notice benefits: improved friendships, reduced stress, and a steady boost in how you see yourself. And when kindness becomes part of your natural habits, you spread a gentle influence wherever you go.

CHAPTER 20: LONG-TERM STRATEGIES

We have spent the entire book talking about how to treat yourself better, let go of harmful thoughts, build healthy relationships, and expand your sense of self-worth. Now it is time to bring these ideas together into long-term strategies that can guide you for years to come. Life does not stand still, and self-improvement is not a one-time task. It is a continuous path. This chapter will look at how to keep the lessons you have learned active, even when life gets tough or changes drastically.

1. Reviewing Core Principles

1. **Self-Acceptance**
   Understanding your strengths and weaknesses, and respecting yourself regardless. This allows you to face your needs and feelings without constant shame.
2. **Healthy Mindset**
   Replacing harsh, negative self-talk with more balanced thoughts. Recognizing mistakes as part of learning, not as proof of worthlessness.
3. **Daily Actions**
   Embracing small habits that support your growth, such as short exercise, simple reading, or checking in with your emotions.
4. **Boundaries and Respect**
   Knowing your limits, saying "no" when needed, and relating to others in a way that respects both sides.
5. **Kindness and Forgiveness**
   Practicing gentle actions toward yourself and others. Learning to let go of anger or grudges to create a healthier emotional space.
6. **Hope and Resilience**
   Finding ways to stay hopeful during hard times, looking for solutions, and bouncing back from setbacks.

As you go forward, you can treat these as guiding lights. Whenever confusion or stress hits, you can revisit these ideas to stay on track.

2. Understanding Change as a Constant

Life goes through phases—school, jobs, relationships, health changes, and more. When a big shift happens, it can unsettle your routines and mindsets. A few tips for handling changes:

1. **Stay Flexible**
   Recognize that a method or habit that worked last year may need adjusting now. This is not a failure; it is a normal response to new conditions.
2. **Use Transitions to Reflect**
   When a big change occurs—like moving to a new place—take a moment to think, "How can I carry my healthy habits here? What might need a tweak?"
3. **Keep Core Routines**
   If possible, hold on to a few simple daily actions no matter the change. These can anchor you, offering familiarity in unfamiliar situations.
4. **Seek New Support**
   If you move or change jobs, find people or groups who share your interests. Building fresh connections helps you stay motivated.

3. Creating a Personal Mission Statement

It can be helpful to write down a short statement about who you want to be and what you stand for. This does not have to be fancy. For example:

> "I am someone who treats myself with respect, learns from mistakes, and offers kindness to others when I can."

Place this statement where you see it daily—on your phone's wallpaper or pinned to a wall. Reading it often can remind you of your goals when you feel lost.

4. Setting Evolving Goals

As you grow, your aims will evolve. You might have short-term and long-term goals. Try the following process:

1. **Reflect**
   Check where you are now. What are you curious about? What do you want to improve?
2. **Decide on a Few Goals**
   Ensure they are realistic. You can have a bigger dream (like learning a new skill deeply) alongside smaller daily goals (like practicing 10 minutes).
3. **Review Regularly**
   Every month or quarter, ask yourself if these goals still make sense. Maybe you need to adjust them or add new ones.
4. **Celebrate Milestones**
   When you hit a milestone, let yourself feel proud. This encourages you to keep aiming forward.

---

5. Building a Support Network

Humans are social creatures, and self-growth often works better with support. Some ways to maintain a helpful social circle:

1. **Stay in Touch with Uplifting People**
   Make time for friends or mentors who encourage your progress and treat you with respect.
2. **Join Groups**
   Whether it is a community class, an online forum, or a local meetup, connecting with like-minded people can provide motivation and new ideas.
3. **Limit Harmful Contacts**
   If someone constantly drags you down or mocks your growth efforts, consider spending less time with them. Setting healthy distance can protect your mindset.
4. **Seek Guidance**
   If you face a big decision, do not hesitate to ask advice from people you trust—family, professionals, or wise peers.

6. Handling Life's Surprises with Adaptability

No plan can predict everything. You might face sudden losses, accidents, or global events that change your life quickly. To handle such surprises:

1. **Ground Yourself**
   In times of chaos, return to basics: breathe deeply, keep small routines going, and talk to someone supportive.
2. **Practice Self-Compassion**
   Do not blame yourself for events you cannot control. Remind yourself you are doing your best in a tough moment.
3. **Break Problems into Steps**
   If a big challenge appears, tackle it piece by piece. Large issues are less overwhelming when handled in smaller parts.
4. **Stay Open to Help**
   Crisis is not the time to isolate. Reaching out can bring resources and emotional comfort. Others often want to help, but might not know how unless you let them in.

---

7. Taking Stock Periodically

Every so often—maybe every 6 months or a year—pause to see how your life is going:

- **What Has Improved?**
  Check if your mindset is kinder to yourself. Notice if you have cut down on negative self-talk.
- **What Feels Stuck?**
  Identify areas where you still feel low or keep repeating old patterns.
- **What Steps Worked Best?**
  Reflect on which habits or strategies truly helped you. Keep these going.
- **What Could You Refine?**
  Maybe a certain approach needs updating or you want to add something fresh to your routine.

This personal check-up keeps you from drifting and helps you stay aligned with the person you aim to be.

8. Avoiding Perfectionism in the Long Term

While striving to grow, watch out for perfectionism—thinking you must do everything flawlessly or you are a failure. This mindset can lead to burnout and shame. Strategies to avoid this trap include:

1. **Plan for Breaks**
   Give yourself days off from strict routines. This keeps them sustainable.
2. **Forgive Slip-Ups**
   If you miss a habit or lose your temper, see it as a small detour, not a reason to quit.
3. **Focus on Trends, Not Single Events**
   Look at your general progress over weeks or months, rather than one "bad day" or "bad moment."
4. **Celebrate Partial Success**
   Recognize small improvements. If your goal was to practice a skill 5 days a week but you only managed 3, that is still better than 0.

---

9. Maintaining a Balanced Lifestyle

Over the long term, it is helpful to keep a sense of balance among different parts of life:

1. **Physical Health**
   Continue some form of movement, balanced eating, and enough sleep. Your body's state affects your emotions and thoughts.
2. **Emotional Health**
   Keep up positive self-talk, journaling, or talking to supportive friends. Mental well-being can dip if neglected.
3. **Relationships**
   Stay connected to people who matter. Make time for fun, honest chats, or shared activities.
4. **Personal Interests**
   Keep exploring hobbies or creative outlets. They can bring joy and a sense of discovery.

5. **Purpose/Contribution**
   If you can, find ways to help in your community or beyond. Feeling useful supports a healthy self-image.

---

10. Updating Your Self-Image as You Grow

As you practice healthy habits, you might notice changes in how you see yourself. Perhaps you have always viewed yourself as shy, but you now speak up more. Or maybe you thought you were "bad at managing money," but you have developed a small savings routine.

1. **Acknowledge Growth**
   Say, "I used to avoid social events, but now I volunteer at a community group. I've changed."
2. **Avoid Old Labels**
   Labels like "I'm lazy" can trap you in old thinking. Replace them with factual statements like, "I'm learning to manage my time better."
3. **Stay Open to New Skills**
   Even if you have never been good at something, you can still improve. Do not limit yourself by old judgments.

---

11. Recognizing Signs of Burnout or Regression

Sometimes you might feel yourself slipping back into negative patterns. Signs can include:

- **Frequent Negative Self-Talk**: You catch yourself calling yourself names again.
- **Avoiding Routines**: You skip the healthy habits you used to do.
- **Irritability or Hopelessness**: Small things bother you a lot, or you feel down for days.
- **Isolation**: You pull away from friends or supportive communities.

If you notice these signs, do not panic. Instead:

1. **Pause**
   Take a break and see what might be causing stress or negativity.
2. **Revisit Basics**
   Go back to the key habits: small daily actions, positive self-talk, or a short walk.
3. **Talk to Someone**
   Sharing your struggles can help you find a path forward.

12. Keeping a Growth Journal or Log

You might find it helpful to maintain a simple notebook or digital file where you record:

- **Goals**: List current targets—both small and big.
- **Progress**: Jot down wins each week or month.
- **Challenges**: Note obstacles you faced and how you managed them.
- **Reflections**: Any insight about your mindset or emotions.

Reviewing this log helps you see patterns and remember how far you have come. It can also serve as motivation during low periods.

13. The Power of Ongoing Learning

Learning should not end once you finish formal schooling or master a basic skill. Keep exploring:

- **Read Books**: On topics like psychology, self-care, or any interest that sparks your curiosity.
- **Attend Workshops**: If there are seminars or events in your area about mental well-being or skill-building, consider going.
- **Learn from Peers**: People around you might have wisdom, whether older relatives or friends with different life experiences.
- **Online Tutorials**: From cooking to finances, many resources are free and can help you expand your abilities.

Staying curious and open to learning leads to continuous growth over the long term.

14. Checking in on Values

Values can shift as life changes. What mattered most to you at one stage might become less central in another. For instance, if you once valued adventure highly, you might shift to valuing stability more when you start a family or take on new responsibilities.

- **Reevaluate Periodically**: Ask, "Which values are most important to me right now?"
- **Adjust Goals to Fit**: If family is now your top value, you might spend more time connecting at home. If creativity is rising in importance, you might schedule daily creative time.
- **Share with Key People**: If you have a partner or close friends, let them know how your values or focus might be changing. This can help them understand new behaviors or priorities.

---

15. Using Technology Wisely

In the modern world, phones and apps can be both a distraction and a tool. For long-term growth:

- **Limit Doom-Scrolling**: Constantly reading bad news or negative commentary can wear you down. Set limits on apps that bring distress without real benefit.
- **Use Reminders**: Apps can remind you of daily actions, track habits, or guide meditation. Make technology a helper, not a stressor.
- **Online Communities**: Carefully choose supportive or skill-building groups rather than places filled with insults or endless arguments.

---

16. Celebrating Milestones

When you reach a certain milestone—like a month of consistent healthy eating, finishing a course, or learning to manage your anger better—reward yourself:

- **Enjoy a Small Treat**: It might be a nice meal, a new book, or a fun day trip.
- **Tell Supporters**: Let friends or family know. Their encouragement can add to your sense of accomplishment.
- **Reflect on the Process**: How did you manage to reach this milestone? What helped? This reflection can boost your confidence in tackling the next goal.

---

17. Serving as a Mentor or Guide

One way to deepen your own understanding is to teach what you have learned. If someone in your life is struggling with self-doubt or negative thinking, you can:

1. **Listen**
   Hear them out without rushing to fix everything.
2. **Share Personal Insights**
   Talk about how you dealt with harsh self-talk or fear of mistakes.
3. **Suggest Simple Steps**
   Recommend small daily actions, a helpful book, or a supportive community.
4. **Stay Supportive, Not Bossy**
   They need to walk their own path. Offer help but let them choose how to use it.

By guiding others, you also remind yourself of the principles you value.

---

18. Staying True to Yourself Despite External Pressure

Society, family, or media might push you to meet certain standards—look a certain way, follow a certain career, or reach a particular status. While it is okay to listen to advice, never lose your own voice:

- **Know Your Inner Compass**: Remember your personal values and goals.

- **Be Open but Filtered**: Consider useful ideas from others but politely discard what clashes too strongly with who you want to be.
- **Stand up for Yourself**: If pressured to do something that feels wrong, it is fine to say, "That's not for me," or "I have a different goal."

---

19. Keeping Hope Alive

Even with all these tools, life can throw challenges that shake your confidence. During very hard moments:

1. **Recall Past Victories**
   Remember times you overcame problems. This memory can spark hope that you can do it again.
2. **Seek Encouragement**
   If you feel you cannot see the positive side, talk to someone who can remind you of your strengths or possibilities.
3. **Focus on One Small Step**
   Instead of trying to fix everything at once, do the next small thing that might help.
4. **Believe in Change**
   Sometimes, you have to hold onto the idea that circumstances can shift, or you can adapt to them, even if it is not clear how right now.

---

20. Combining Self-Kindness with Discipline

Long-term success involves balancing compassion for yourself with the discipline to keep going. Some ways to balance these:

- **Set Realistic Schedules**: Aim to do tasks and follow routines, but allow flexibility for rest or unexpected events.
- **Speak Kindly to Motivate**: Instead of pushing yourself with insults ("Get up, you lazy person!"), encourage yourself with firm but gentle language ("Let's do this step now, I believe I can handle it.").
- **Adjust Goals if Life Changes**: If new duties appear—like caring for a relative—alter your schedule in a balanced way.

- **Reward Hard Work**: Allow yourself small joys after focused periods of effort.

---

21. Planning for Future Dreams

It helps to think about your life in broader terms sometimes—where do you see yourself in a few years? This does not have to be rigid. It is more about direction:

- **Create a Vision Board or List**: Include personal growth aims (e.g., "be more patient"), skill goals ("learn guitar"), relationship hopes ("strengthen bond with family"), or career dreams.
- **Break Down Into Steps**: Even big dreams can start with simple actions. If you want to travel overseas, the first step might be reading about places or saving a small amount monthly.
- **Stay Open to Adjustments**: As you try new things, your idea of the future might shift. That is natural.

---

22. Reflection and Gratitude

Over the long term, practicing reflection and gratitude can keep your mind balanced. Each day or week:

- **Note 1-3 Things You Appreciated**: They can be small joys, like a tasty meal or a warm conversation.
- **Reflect on Lessons**: If something went wrong, quickly jot what you learned, so it does not become a lingering regret.
- **Share Gratitude**: Let people know if you value their support. This can deepen your connections.

23. Knowing When to Seek Professional Help

There may be times when personal growth methods and friendly support are not enough—like if you struggle with persistent sadness, anxiety, or overwhelming thoughts. A mental health professional, counselor, or doctor can provide specialized guidance. Seeking help is a sign of strength, not weakness. It shows you care about your well-being enough to get expert insight.

---

24. Recognizing Your Ongoing Journey

You will not wake up one day and say, "I'm fully done growing—everything is perfect now!" Growth keeps unfolding through all stages of life. There might be times you feel on top of the world and other times you face new challenges. Continue:

- **Being Patient**: Growth can be slow, with ups and downs.
- **Adapting**: As you learn more about yourself, tweak your routines and goals.
- **Staying Humble**: No matter how much you improve, remain open to new lessons.
- **Helping Others Along the Way**: Growth is sweeter when shared. If you learn something helpful, pass it on.

---

25. A Final Encouragement

You have covered a lot of ground in this book, from self-acceptance to dealing with negativity, from building better boundaries to practicing kindness. You have looked at ways to forgive yourself and others, to manage stress and worry, to create daily habits that build confidence, and to learn from your mistakes. These are not separate lessons but parts of a whole approach to liking who you are, growing steadily, and connecting positively with the world around you.

The journey ahead will bring chances to apply what you have learned. There will be mistakes and triumphs, slow days and energetic bursts. Through it all, remember that you deserve kindness—from yourself and others—and that real change often comes in small, steady steps. Trust that you can keep learning, keep adapting, and keep caring for yourself in a way that leads to a deeper sense of worth. With patience, openness, and these strategies, you can continue to love yourself and grow for the rest of your life. Take these insights, keep them close, and allow yourself the grace to move forward, day by day.

Congratulations on reading through these chapters. Here's to a future where you fully accept and care for who you are, while also reaching out with kindness, resilience, and hope to all around you. This is the ongoing, beautiful path of personal growth.

End of the Book

You have completed "How to Love Myself: A Self Help Book for Self-Acceptance and Personal Growth." Remember that the real work happens as you apply these ideas in small, daily ways. Be patient with yourself. Enjoy the journey of growth. And whenever you feel uncertain, come back to these pages to remind yourself that you are worthy of love and capable of steady progress—one step at a time.

www.ingramcontent.com/pod-product-compliance
Lightning Source LLC
LaVergne TN
LVHW012043070526
838202LV00056B/5583